The Ins   ᴜᴄᴋ

Nick

Best Wishes

Jeremy

Jeremy Glyn
AIPTI, FKF, ICRP

ISBN Number 9781849149402

Revised edition printed in Great Britain by
Lightning Source International
February 2017

Cover by Nicole Wells,
Graphic Designer, Webkick Ltd

For Theo, and others like him, who inspire us to recognise how much more we could do.

I am enormously grateful to the many people who have helped me with the writing, proofreading, and production of this book, not least David Hemery C.B.E. who took the time and trouble to offer me suggestions, and corrections, that have improved it considerably.

Contents

Endorsements of coaching sessions and workshops that Jeremy has facilitated

Coaching endorsements:

"The subconscious is an often untapped resource in the world of sports psychology. Jeremy's integrated approach takes sports psychology to a new and even more powerful level. I would recommend Jeremy to any competitor at any level wishing to achieve their full potential.

What interests me, more than just the psychology side of what he does, is the kinesiology, which is really interesting, in that you get right to the nub of what your worries, concerns, and fears might be, as you are really tapping into your subconscious.

So at the end of the session, you know you've dealt with the problems that you need to, if you're going to perform to the best of your ability."

Goldie Sayers,
British women's javelin record holder 2016

"What you told me was very important. I now understand the significance of visualising success and will start doing mental preparation. 'Mindset Priming' was very relevant to me in helping me achieve my goals and objectives and I am keen to have a follow-up session soon."

Sean Safo-Antwi,
One of Britain's top 100 metres sprinters

"When I started working with Jeremy I was a top-level amateur golfer and my goal was to turn pro and play to the highest level. In the first two weeks from when he started mentoring me, I reduced my golf handicap from 1.8 to 0.6 and was soon able to turn pro and realise my goal.

With Jeremy the main thing was controlling emotions, and controlling the 'little voice between the ears'. In golf it's really, really important.

I've recommended Jeremy to various people and to other competitors, though I wouldn't want to give too much away to fellow competitors, to give them an edge, but I would 100% recommend him."

Darren Lovegrove,
Golf professional

"Jeremy enabled me to go straight to the core of a number of problems that were holding me back in life. Of all the approaches I tried, I found his by far the most effective. I'm most grateful to him."

J.B.,
Solicitor, Devon

"Thank you so much for the time you spent with me! I was fascinated by your methods, and quite astounded by the clarity and insight it gave me into issues that had remained uncleared in my own subconscious.

I am enthused about how this can be brought into my own coaching practice, as I continue to grow and develop my offering to my own clients. If ever an opportunity arose to work together, I would relish it!"

Cathy Richardson, FInstSMM
Master Coach and Keynote Speaker
Cathy Richardson Associates

'Mindset Priming' was hugely relevant to me in achieving my goals. I have now set myself more ambitious targets and I'm very keen to have a later session to see if I can stretch my goals further. The sessions have unblocked my inner self-belief, removed negative energy, and given me a clear mindset."

Reece Prescod,
19-year-old 200 metres runner

"Jeremy uses his techniques to amazing effect. I can confirm that my 17-year-old dyslexic son's life, and my own, have been speedily turned around."

Nicola Martin,
Principal, Institute of Clinical Hypnosis

"I want to thank you so much Jeremy for such amazing work and would without a shadow of doubt highly recommend you and work with you again myself. I left feeling uplifted and so clear about my goals and clear that now nothing stands in my way with my resistance levels to zero."

Marie Hubbard,
Personal Trainer

"I liked the 'Mindset Priming' sessions and now I am more open to the idea of running faster than I think I can! I also recognise that I don't need to be the favourite in order to win. I am keen to have a later coaching session to see if I could stretch my goals and also to attend a workshop on mental preparation for success – meanwhile I will stop trying to coerce myself into being successful."

Jordan Kirby,
22-year-old 200 metres runner

9

Workshop endorsements:

"This has had a significant impact on my understanding of leadership, and on my attitude to it. It has transformed my thinking and application and has led to fantastic results."
Bob Skinstad,
Captain, South African Rugby Union 1998-2002
World Cup winning squad member 2007

"You have opened my eyes to practical applications of concepts I have been working with for 30 years. I now see how they relate to my marriage, my children, my health, my hobbies and the way I run my business – I am absolutely gobsmacked."
Stein Jatten,
Senior Partner, Human Link,
Psychological consultancy, Norway

"I recommend Jeremy as a bright professional; personable, expert, with high integrity, and the ability to help people understand their areas for improvement and development. I appreciated his special way to make me see things from a different perspective."
Domenico Traverso,
Managing Director, GKN Axles, Italy

"This mentoring approach will enable me to raise the self-esteem of others in the organisation and give people the opportunity to undertake tasks I previously would have been reluctant to assign them."
Harry Hone,
Production Manager, Brita Finish

"I found the insights you teach very helpful. Your course has furnished me with a few missing key points which I see as essential for proper understanding. I would recommend your courses to anyone who wants to improve themselves or their performance, and tell them no-one teaches this information as clearly as you do."
Christine Green, Hypnotherapist,
Partner, the Wellbeing Consultancy

"Since your input, attitudes have really changed in the company. Previously reserved and reticent people are now standing up and becoming accountable. We have developed a 'can do' mentality combined with a 'want to' attitude. No other management approach has come within 50% of this."
Raymond Elderton,
Head of Training, Keepmoat Holdings

"I found Jeremy's way of teaching very inspiring. To have 'creative avoidance' highlighted, and to be given tools to stop avoiding issues was brilliant. I shall no longer put a ceiling on my way of thinking."
Caroline Hall,
Helping Hands in Tadley

"By using what I learned I moved up from number 25 salesman in 1999, to number 2 salesman in 2000 with 192,000 points. Until then the highest total for a full year had been 265,000 points. So far in 2001 I am top salesman, with 560,000 points, bringing in IR£ 2.25 million of annual new business already this year."
Jim Barry,
Executive Financial Advisor,
Canada Life Insurance, Ireland

"Jeremy you provided me with the most concentrated yet helpful course I believe I will ever have in my career. It would be good to keep in touch, thanks – Pete"
Pete Hewitt,
Supply Chain Manager, GKN OffHighway

"Thank you for the invaluable and eye-opening information I learnt from attending the workshop, especially the information about 'self-talk'. I received a massive insight about myself and the huge impact 'self-talk' has had on my life and success. I urge anyone who has not been on one of Jeremy's workshops to do so."
Marie Hubbard,
Personal Trainer

"These 'insights' will address our issues by turning negative thinkers into positive and by releasing more of our human resource potential."
Knut Am,
President PPCo, Norway

"The techniques introduced could prove to be that extra dimension underpinning the success of this and future projects."
Peter Dukas,
Senior Project Manager,
Courtaulds Engineering

"Jeremy you are so lucky. Everyone would benefit from this approach."
Bill Curral,
Group Financial Controller, GKN plc (2004)

"This is very powerful stuff, it is superb and could help everyone!"
John Boffey,
Managing Director, Wyken Tools

"These concepts filled a whole gap in my education. I now set more ambitious targets, for myself and the business, and know how to achieve them."
Johnny Blackstone,
Managing Director, Blackstone Builders

"Jeremy has supported me for over 20 years. Since he introduced this approach to a GKN Division sales nearly doubled, the operating profit trebled and the value of the business quadrupled in four years."
Martyn Vaughan,
Group Director of Enterprise Excellence, GKN

"Great workshop – Jeremy always motivates and encourages me to work harder to achieve my goals and to change the way I think. I will change my habits and beliefs and move my company forward to achieve my business goals."
Bhupinder Ghatahora,
Ghatahora Photography

"I believe your form of teaching is essential in making champions. It helped me and my team to develop a hugely successful business because it enables ordinary people to do extraordinary things."
Terry G. Bramall,
Chairman, Keepmoat plc (1990-2000)

About the author

I never imagined, 30 years ago, that I would find myself working with Olympic competitors, running workshops for sports psychologists and coaches, and mentoring aspiring sports stars, individuals, parents, business leaders and organisations, to achieve great things. I just set out to deal with some issues, and develop my understanding of how mental preparation can unleash potential.

In my mid-thirties, having sold my share in a business I had co-founded in 1975, I became interested in the many benefits to be gained from working with complementary therapies, and kinesiology in particular.

In the mid-1980s, after training with Gordon Stokes and Daniel Whiteside in the USA, I started teaching people in Europe how to help those with dyslexia using the 3-in-1 Concepts kinesiology approach. Since then I've also worked with adults and children, helping them to set realistic goals and develop their self-belief.

I studied a range of therapies and approaches, including Neuro Linguistic Programming (NLP) and Jose Siva's 'mind control', and was then introduced to the work of Lou Tice of The Pacific Institute®. They had developed a range of training programmes that incorporated many of the concepts that I had previously encountered and found helpful.

I was impressed that the institute's approach could be used in organisations, in prisons, in schools and colleges, and also with unemployed or disadvantaged people in communities.

For over 30 years, as an associate and project director for them, I have run corporate seminars and workshops, on the 'Psychology of Success' and raising aspirations. This has helped many business leaders transform their organisations and unleash the potential of their people.

I decided some years ago to call my own corporate and coaching business 'Pathfinders', after the planes and pilots in the Second World War that helped others to get from their starting point to their chosen destination – for that summed up what my approach enabled me to do for my clients.

I was keen to help individuals as well, and after being trained as a coach by David Hemery (Olympic gold medallist), I began working with private clients as a coach/mentor/holistic therapist and mind trainer.

I read and studied extensively and, as I became more and more aware of how the mind works, I was able to integrate what I learnt about psychology with the kinesiological concepts I was using.

Now that the approach has been thoroughly tried and tested with athletes at an elite level, I am sharing these concepts and models with other mentors so that many more people can work with it, and benefit from it.

I take every opportunity to give talks, run 'Escalating Coaching' workshops, and teach those who want to use this approach to work with their clients at a deeper level.

As I see it, the more coaches, sports psychologists, and kinesiologists I can inspire to adopt this approach, the more clients they will get, and the more fulfilled and successful their clients will be.

I am looking for kinesiologists, and coaches who want to gain the ability to explain the practical applications of the psychological element.

I also hope that many coaches will choose to gain the simple kinesiological techniques that will enable them to help their clients at a much deeper level.

I have no intention of retiring – I am enjoying my work, and the rewards it gives me and those I help, far too much!

The author's £1,000 challenge

I recognise that my challenge is to gain credibility, for my integrated approach, among elite sports stars and their coaches.

I also recognise that until you have experienced the 'Mindset Priming' process for yourself, you can neither imagine how easily it works nor how reliable it is.

To encourage you to put my claims to the test I have decided to put my money where my mouth is.

My challenge to you is this:

I am so convinced that you are currently limiting your aspirations, and (subconsciously) limiting your success, that I will pay £1,000 (to be shared equally between you and your coach) if you are the first UK competitor I have encountered who has already set their optimum target and is not inhibiting their success.

So – give me the chance to introduce my approach to you, preferably with your coach in attendance.

I will hopefully be able to show you that your subconscious self-belief, in what you could achieve in your sport, is greater than your current goals.

I will hopefully also be able to identify for you the amount of subconscious resistance you currently have to fulfilling your potential.

I may also be able to reduce, if not fully remove your subconscious resistance to achieving your goals.

You have nothing to lose (I will test you for free) and potentially £1,000 to win.

To apply please submit your request on my website: www.pathfindersabc.co.uk.

Part 1
Introduction

"The physical aspect of the sport can only take you so far.

The mental aspect has to kick in, especially when you're talking about the best of the best.

In the Olympic Games, everyone is talented.

Everyone trains hard.

Everyone does the work.

What separates the gold medallists from the silver medallists is simply the mental game."

Shannon Miller,
Olympic gold medal winning gymnast

The origins of this book

Having developed this very powerful approach, that integrates kinesiology and psychology, I have often said "if I were to die without having taught other people how to use the approach, it would be a terrible waste".

The decision to get writing was given some urgency when talking with Olympic medallists Steve Backley and Roger Black (both of whom had greatly benefitted from kinesiological support).

Roger told me, "The man who helped me with kinesiology was very old, and he died before he could write a book". He then looked me up and down (I considered myself to be 69 years young at the time) and continued "You'd better start writing!".

On the one hand, they told me I needed to produce a book alerting athletes, aspiring sports stars, and their coaches to the 'Mindset Priming' process that would enable them to raise their aspirations, and expectations, by putting them in touch with their inner self-belief. On the other hand, they commented that over the last ten years the support given to athletes and competitors in this vital area had greatly deteriorated (at least in the UK).

With their encouragement, and support, I began using this integrated approach with both Olympic, and Paralympic, competitors and prospects, with the aim of boosting their successes in the 2016 Games in Rio and in the World Championships in London in 2017.

My 'ABC of Success' model

I created the 'ABC' model to help my clients to look at the interactions between their Aspirations, their current Behaviour, their Conditioning and their Description of themselves.

The model illustrates the key elements involved in the three stages of progressing from your current levels of performance to your preferred standard.

There are inevitably a great many concepts that interact with each other in the complex field of Cognitive psychology. I found it hard to present them in a coherent form until I developed the 'ABC of Success' and 'Pinnacle of Success' models in the late 1990s.

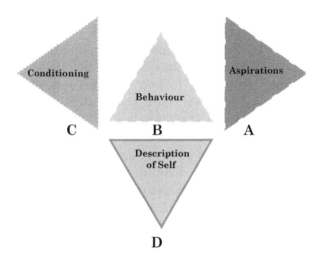

At a simple level the models help you understand the need to address the underlying reasons that you get 'stuck' at your current, or below par, levels of performance. I am convinced that when you understand and apply the concepts for yourself you will have a far better chance of achieving success.

I am persuaded that far too few people understand that the simplest and most comfortable way to get to 'A' (whatever you are aspiring to) from 'B' (your current behaviour or performance level) is to focus on 'C' (your conditioning) and 'D' (your subconscious description of yourself).

I have come across very few people who have the knowledge and techniques required to really focus on 'D'

– which is probably the most critical element of the change process.

For now, I will just ask you to focus on the fact that the model illustrates that your free-flowing behaviour will be driven by your inner description of yourself. It follows that sustainable (and comfortable) change is best achieved by initially adjusting that inner description, and then letting the behaviour progressively follow.

The purpose of this book

After a talk I gave, on the 'ABC of Success' model, a former international table tennis player told me that I should not only be working with athletes and other competitors but should also be training our Olympic coaches.

I recognised that my approach would indeed give an added dimension not only to Olympic, but particularly Paralympic, and Invictus Games coaches (for reasons I will expand on in Part 3). The more I thought about it, it dawned on me that 'Mindset Priming' would also add value to sports psychologists working with competitors across every conceivable sporting endeavour.

I have given numerous talks and presentations in Europe and the U.S.A. and members of the audience have frequently asked if they could buy 'my book'. Thanks to Roger I realised that it was indeed about time I wrote it.

This book is therefore primarily for aspiring sports stars, coaches, and sports psychologists, though it will also give valuable insights to any individual (whether a life coach, student, parent, employer, employee, or retired person) wanting to use more of their potential, or to be more fulfilled.

I stress it is *not* intended to be a 'self-help' book!

23

Having hopefully made that clear, Part 2 of this book, the Psychology part, covers many well-known concepts that all readers will be able to use to their advantage.

Part 4 is deliberately all about what each of you can do for yourselves, to use more of your potential and fulfil your ambitions. Also the last chapter of Part 4, 'Mental simulation', is in the free 'Mind Games' download, on the website, as an immediately available resource for athletes, or for anyone who is looking for support of this kind.

My main message in the book is that, if you really want to stretch yourself and fulfil your heartfelt ambitions, you are likely to need help, from a suitably qualified coach, to tap into your inner aspirations, and then to overcome any lurking, subconscious, doubts about your prospects of making your dreams come true.

Since starting to run my workshops for individuals, sports stars, and coaches, my students have in turn mentored me to raise my own sights. They have helped me to recognise that 'Mindset Priming' will not just benefit individuals but also teams, not only be valuable to sports coaches but also to personal trainers and life coaches.

I have found their excitement to be infectious and I am working to ensure my own mindset is appropriate to work at the highest level to do justice to this approach and all those who could benefit from it.

Research on success

Diagnosing the root causes of underperformance

It is well recognised that those who do win very often start with a strong belief that they *can* win. The issue that most coaches, and sports psychologists, are ill-equipped to deal with is how to raise a competitor's self-belief in their ability, and their prospects of winning, to the optimum level.

My blend of kinesiology and psychology is the most fabulously effective approach to help coaches, in every field of endeavour, to address this key issue and it is especially appropriate for those working in competitive sports.

Self-efficacy (one's belief in what one can achieve in a specific area) was the subject of research by Professor Albert Bandura, of Stanford University, who is probably the most respected psychologist alive today doing research on high performance individuals and organisations. He suggests that to address the root cause(s) of our underperformance we need to assess the extent to which our Conditioning (Culture in an organisation), Competence, and Commitment are appropriate for the task ahead.

Seeking commitment

The following diagram illustrates his research into what he sees as the key elements of commitment, self-motivation and self-efficacy (an individual's or organisation's belief in what they are able to achieve), in the context of sustaining high performance:

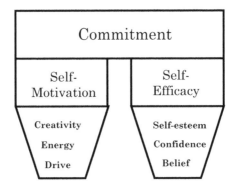

Bandura's research suggests what the ingredients of commitment are (creativity, energy, drive, confidence, self-esteem and belief) yet the chances are that, like the vast majority of those who have attended my workshops in businesses all over the Northern hemisphere, you will have no idea how to generate or develop those elements for yourself, your team mates, your clients, or members of your family.

Most sports coaches and business leaders recognise the significance of increasing commitment as a key to progress, yet are ill-equipped to do so.

Developing commitment

To give a competitor the best mental preparation to excel, my suggestion would be that the essential first stage is to put them in touch with the self-belief, in their potential, that is lurking unrecognised in their unconscious mind.

The second stage is to identify, and demonstrably remove, any doubts about their ability lodged in the back of their mind.

The third stage is to make sure they understand how their mind works, and how they can 'put their mind to' achieving their goals. I provide in-depth answers on how to do that in my workshops, but will introduce the key elements to you in this book. For now, I will just flag up that the answer lies in you understanding, and applying, what I am going to refer to as 'mind games'.

One 'mind game' is the key to generating your drive, energy, and creativity, the ingredients of self-motivation, and a different 'mind game' can be used to develop your belief, self-esteem, and confidence, the ingredients of your self-efficacy, which is so essential if you are to be at your best at the highest level of any competition.

Perhaps the most important 'mind games' for an athlete are those that change your inner self-image, and thereby raise your performance comfort zone to a new level, making it easier for you to get 'in the zone' when competing in an elite event.

Since the 'mind games' I am referring to were explained to me, and I understood not only how to use them effectively but also, importantly, why they would work, I have successfully improved many aspects of my life and know they will help you in whatever aspect(s) of your life you choose to apply them.

Pioneering a new approach

Imagine for a moment that you are a sports competitor, and that you can open an app on your phone, or computer, that invites you to enter both your best performance to date, and the performance level you are trying to achieve.

How amazing and eye-opening would it be if you could then scroll down the page (as if you were progressing from your conscious thoughts, through your subconscious, to the unconscious level of your mind) and be shown your inner self-belief of what you can achieve?

What would it do for your confidence and commitment if you could then scroll left on the screen, and firstly be shown any doubts, reservations and mental demons that might be holding you back from success, and secondly, after some help from your coach, be able to see they had been totally deleted for you?

I don't know of an app that will let you do this, but I have developed an approach I call 'Escalating Coaching' that achieves precisely what I have described.

The approach has several levels of skill. 'Mindset Priming' is the collective name for the basic processes which establish your inner self-belief in how high you could set your goal, identify what level of resistance, or subconscious sabotage, exists to that aspiration, then reduce (if not necessarily remove) that resistance, and finally, importantly, fine-tune the most appropriate 'mind game(s)' that will help you achieve your ambition.

'Mind/Body Alignment' is the name of the more profound process that goes beyond what 'Mindset Priming' achieves. It demonstrably removes any resistance to your success lurking at the back of your mind, and also 'balances' all your energy levels, thereby improving your mental and physical alignment with your goal.

Developing these two combinations of kinesiology and psychology enabled me to address the fact that most of my clients, including successful sports stars, were unwittingly setting targets and aspirations well within their potential, and well below their ideal picture of their future.

It also helped me with the other essential aspects of preparing a competitor for elite success – demonstrably removing doubts lurking at the back of their mind and teaching them how to get 'in the zone'.

Every Olympic and Paralympic prospect that I have worked with so far has immediately been able to raise their expectations of success with my approach.

To my astonishment none of them had been taught how to prepare themselves mentally for that level of success.

If you are a coach, I am really keen to share the techniques with you, whether you are working with sports stars, business leaders or private individuals. This book will alert you to a more profound way of working that gives you access to your clients' unconscious goals and challenges and will complement your existing skills and techniques.

If you are a sports psychologist, I hope the book will prompt you to gain the simple techniques that will complement your work and enable you to take it to a deeper (subconscious) level.

If you are already a trained therapist, it will be simple for you to add the understanding of the psychological concepts, and kinesiological techniques, to the menu of what you already offer clients.

If you are an athlete and hope to compete in the European Championships, the next Olympics, the Paralympics, the Invictus Games, or the World Championships, then this book is written for you, for your coach, and for your sports psychologist.

If you play golf, or any sport competitively, then read on if you want to know, like the sports stars I have helped, how to discover your inner beliefs about what you could achieve and to progress towards improving your levels of performance.

If you are someone striving to achieve more of your potential, this book will introduce you to key concepts and tools you can use on your own to make the changes in your life.

I hope that it will also encourage you to get the external support you need, whether your ideal goal is to achieve sporting stardom or to lead a happier, more fulfilling and more successful life.

If you are already mentoring others, and want to add to your existing skills, identifying which of these aspects of the process you want to be involved in will establish which of my 'Mindset Priming' workshops are most appropriate for you:

- *Helping clients raise their aspirations to the top limit of their inner self-belief.*

- *Checking for 100% commitment to that goal.*

- *Checking for any subconscious resistance to the pursuit of that goal.*

- *Demonstrably reducing (and maybe removing) subconscious doubts or resistance.*

- *'Balancing' the client's energy systems and removing any subconscious doubts or resistance.*

- *Helping clients to adjust their comfort zone to the new level of achievement.*

- *Identifying the 'mind games' that would accelerate the client's progress.*

It has struck me that there is a parallel to be drawn between what is involved in this approach (coaching someone to progress from where they are now to achieve something they are passionate about) and what is involved in tackling a neglected garden.

The gardener initially gets a picture in their mind of how they would like things to be. Frustratingly (because they will be itching to plant the seeds and shrubs they want to grow) the second important step is to clear all the brambles and weeds and stones from the flowerbeds and ensure the soil is fertile. Only then is it sensible to plant and nurture what is needed to achieve their desired outcome.

Competitors need help to picture their best outcome, to remove the clutter from their minds, to establish a productive mindset, and then to nurture their ambition to the point of success.

Let me give you one last word on the reduction or removal of clutter and resistance. Many years ago I was given the best description I have ever heard of how precise and gentle the 'Mindset Priming' process is.

Helena Bonham Carter's mother, a very highly qualified psychotherapist, came to my London clinic, with Helena, to attend a talk I was giving on my way of working with kinesiology. She had so many questions that she asked if I was available for dinner. The three of us went to a local Fulham restaurant and talked at length about my way of working.

Being nearly 30 years ago, I cannot claim to be word perfect on what she said, but her final words that evening were, as best I can remember, "When trying to get to the root of a client's issues, as a well-trained psychotherapist I carefully ask questions about events in their past, seeking the incidents or trauma that may have triggered the issues that need dealing with. Inevitably, in the process, I disturb uncomfortable memories that have nothing to do with the main problem. With your approach, it sounds as if you go in like a laser to precisely the right spot, zap what needs to be worked on, and come out again without disturbing anything else – I am green with envy".

That really gives you the best picture of how simply and easily the approach worked at that time.

With the added element of the psychological concepts that are now included, it is even more powerful and effective than it was before.

It is my hope and intention that:

All readers will understand more about:
Why people resist change;
How to generate *commitment* to change;
How 'mind games' will let them achieve their goals.

Competitors will understand more about:
How to identify and achieve their *ideal* goals;
What stops people being 'successful';
A way to 'change' or improve performance that is a comfortable process.

Coaches will understand more about:
The 'Psychology of Success';
The benefits of accessing *unconscious* aspirations;
How to remove deep-lying resistance to progress.

Kinesiologists, sports psychologists, sports coaches, and life coaches will understand:
How easily they could gain the knowledge to qualify them to help emerging sports stars, and all their clients, with this combined approach.

Part 2
The Psychology part

"In training everyone focuses on 90% physical and 10% mental, but in competitions it's 90% mental.

The mind is one of the main aspects to succeeding in sport whatever your level."

Sir Ben Ainslie,
Quadruple Olympic gold medallist

Raising the bar

The key points:

Successful people confidently set goals without knowing how they will achieve them.

Your spontaneous decisions are made after a rapid appraisal of your perceptions/memories rather than on reality or your current ability/potential.

Your inner/ideal goals are usually more of a stretch than you are currently aiming for.

Your drive, energy and creativity (to achieve your goals) are best stimulated by having the maximum stretch between your current performance and that which you are aspiring to.

It is possible for suitably trained coaches to put you in touch with not only your subconscious but unconscious level of self-belief about what you can, and ideally would like to, achieve.

If you are already highly successful in your sport, or your career, it is quite likely that you are one of the 15% of people who are instinctively successful. I have learnt that even that elite group are still likely to benefit from learning some practical applications, of the basic psychological concepts that underpin their success, as well as the more profound implications.

I am indebted for that realisation to Bill Curral, who, when I first met him, was chief financial controller of GKN, a highly successful business then employing some 42,000 people.

I shared some of these concepts with him, one to one, over three days and about half way through our sessions he said "You are so lucky, Jeremy, because everybody needs you – the 85% of people who don't use their potential need you because they don't know what to do, and the 15%, who are instinctively successful, need you because they don't know what they're doing".

Even as one of the instinctively successful 15% himself, he recognised that with an in-depth understanding of the concepts you gain the ability, and opportunity, to apply the techniques deliberately, and thereby accelerate your progress towards your objectives.

We all have limited perception

Some people seem to have a clear picture of what they want to achieve in life at an early age. Most of us do not, but progress through life looking for a fulfilling future and perhaps missing opportunities that pass us by without even noticing them.

There many reasons we do not see all there is to see in our environment. Some of the limits to our perception are readily understood from an early age.

We learn that dogs can hear whistles that are silent to the human ear. We see how medical x-rays can see through what appears, to the naked eye, to be solid matter. We understand that infra-red light exposes things invisible to the eye, and that night sights enable users to see in the dark.

If you have ever done any proofreading you are probably well aware that we have a tendency to see what we expect, rather than spot any errors. An extreme example of this occurred when I was having dinner one night in a restaurant in Italy, sitting opposite a corporate client who was proudly wearing his company's latest T-shirt, complete with the organisation's name and logo prominently displayed. Unbelievably it had been printed with the company name spelt wrongly but, because I had expected to see the company name that I knew so well, I had looked at it for some time before I noticed the error (which clearly had not yet been spotted by any of the company's employees either!).

What causes us to have 'blind spots'

It is not only our sense of sight that can be inhibited. What we hear, smell, and feel may also be limited.

Car keys, house keys, glasses, and all sorts of objects that are 'under our noses' (or in a handbag) may become temporarily invisible for reasons that I will be explaining and expanding upon in-depth later.

Some of the strangest examples of 'blind spots' occur when people have developed a very strong, but erroneous, belief about themselves or their abilities.

Beliefs and cognitive dissonance

Leon Festinger developed the theory of cognitive dissonance. At its simplest this very important and significant theory suggests that, when we are confronted by conflicting truths, disharmony occurs.

In extreme cases, when reality is presenting us with evidence that contradicts a very firmly held belief, our subconscious will create a sufficiently powerful 'blind spot' to prevent us consciously recognising that reality. By doing so it protects us from the shock and pain of having one of our fundamental beliefs shattered.

Unfortunately, the consequences of this can be fatal. A potentially tragic example of this is when an anorexic (who KNOWS they are overweight, although matchstick thin) is asked to draw their reflection on a mirror. Though looking at their matchstick self, they draw the shape of the overweight person they so firmly believe themselves to be. Their inability to recognise the reality of their condition is a major barrier to treatment, without which they will die.

I did not fully understand just how powerful this concept could be until a client said the most extraordinary thing I have yet to hear. It remains the most astonishing illustration I have come across of the cognitive dissonance concept.

I had agreed to try and help a very bright 12-year-old boy who was afflicted by severe dyslexia. He had been discarded by the conventional education system, and had also been thrown out of three special schools that had labelled him as 'unmanageable, unteachable and uncontrollable'.

When, having done some work with him, I gave him an exercise to do that involved him saying his alphabet, he stunned me, given how bright he clearly was, by telling me that he wouldn't be able to say his alphabet because he had never been able to learn it.

I encouraged him to show me what he could do and he then (thanks to the session I had had with him) surprised me by reciting the alphabet faultlessly, at an even pace, without any hesitation, from A to Z.

That obviously amazed and delighted me and I naturally congratulated him on having said his alphabet perfectly. I was totally unprepared for his reply: "I didn't, I couldn't have, I don't know it".

He had said his alphabet perfectly, for the first time in his life, and then denied the fact within just a few seconds of having done so.

After learning about cognitive dissonance, I realised that he had built up an unshakeable belief that he did not know his alphabet, from many years of listening to his teachers, his parents, his siblings, his peers (and, as you will come to appreciate, most importantly from listening to himself) saying that he was so unteachable that he could not even learn that. So great was this belief that, for his own protection, his subconscious managed to shield him from the reality that he had, just a moment before, recited the alphabet perfectly.

This cognitive dissonance concept is sometimes referred to as the 'sure enough principle'. This suggests that if you believe something strongly enough, for example that your day will turn out a certain way, then you will unknowingly ignore any evidence that might confront you with the opposite reality. As a result, lo and behold come the end of the day, 'sure enough' you think you have had the day, or result, that you expected.

A more positive application of this theory is that when you are convinced that you are right about something, you will not allow yourself to be limited by the negative input from 'experts'.

One of my clients was involved in a horrendous car crash that smashed both his legs. His doctors tried to persuade him that he would never walk again and that they needed to amputate both legs. They even persuaded his wife to show him the x-rays demonstrating the irreparable damage.

As he had walked into my office unaided, and without any sign of a limp, I was astonished to hear his story. When we discussed cognitive dissonance he said that this concept explained why he had persistently argued with his wife and had insisted, until then, that she had never showed him the x-rays.

His absolute belief (that he would be able to walk again after the accident) had led him not only to reject the advice of the doctors but also to block out the evidence that they had sought to show him.

At an elite sporting level, Goldie Sayers, our top women's javelin thrower for many years, who has competed at an Olympic level since 2004, was told by 'experts' in the early days of her career that she was too small to be a successful javelin thrower. Happily, her self-efficacy was stronger than her respect for her doubters and she went on to become the British record holder and is still competing in the Olympics and World Championships.

Astonishingly, in my experience of working with Olympic stars and prospects, I've discovered that without exception (thus far) even they limit their aspirations. Because no-one had previously put them in touch with their unconscious beliefs in what they could achieve, they had failed to develop their self-efficacy appropriately – and I am pretty sure you would discover the same was true of you.

Aim higher – with confidence

One more key insight for you to appreciate is that it is vital to realise how much you limit your successes if you set your goals based on what you already know 'how to' achieve. Many people feel it is 'unrealistic' to set goals without seeing how it is possible to achieve them.

One very successful managing director, who has employed me to teach these concepts to a succession of six leadership teams in different (and highly profitable) businesses, refuses to allow the word 'realistic' in the boardroom because he fully appreciates the significance of this insight.

You need to understand the function of a filter system in your brain called the Reticular Activating System (RAS).

The RAS is a net-like group of cells that acts like a good executive secretary - it screens out the junk mail, whatever you do not need to see, or know about, at that time. The implication of this is that the environment holds a mass of potentially useful information of which you are blissfully unaware. You can actually look at it without seeing it.

Your senses are bombarded by far more information than you can, or need to, acknowledge at the conscious level. At times, as we saw from the cognitive dissonance examples, you may need to screen out reality from your conscious awareness; at other times it might be of real value to be more aware of the information potentially available to you.

The advertisement that perhaps caught your eye this morning has probably been in your paper every day. The reason you would not have seen it before is that until now you had no need of the item advertised.

The more clearly you know what it is that you are seeking, the easier it is for the RAS to scan for it.

An early experience of the value of the RAS occurred some years ago when my niece asked me if I would be the first person to buy her a camera. She was very clear about the sort of camera she wanted and described it in great and loving detail. I knew the type she meant and, although I personally thought it looked horrible, I was clear that she had set her mind on it and I recognised that it would be a very suitable first camera for her.

I was living in London at the time and set off to walk from my home to a camera shop, with my niece's camera in mind. As I walked along the pavement the shops were on my left and I knew I had only about a quarter of a mile to walk.

I was looking straight ahead of me, ignoring all the shops I was walking past, and focusing on reaching the camera shop. What happened next was all the more remarkable given that my left eye barely functions.

I stopped walking after about 50 yards and entered a chemist's shop on my left. In spite of the limited eyesight in my left eye, my subconscious had registered, thanks to my RAS being primed, that the precise camera I was looking for was sitting in the shop window.

Your RAS filters information from all of your senses, not just the sense of sight, and not just when you are awake.

On one of the first workshops that I ran, a mother got quite irate when I suggested that the reason she woke in the night, if her baby cried, was because it was her responsibility to do so and therefore the sound got through to her conscious awareness. She insisted it was no more than her maternal instinct that made her wake up.

Happily for me a nanny was also on the course and she described her role in helping couples who both needed a good night's sleep. She told the group that once she had accepted accountability for the welfare of the baby her filter system was primed to alert her to any cry in the night. As a result both parents were able to sleep soundly (their filters effectively switched off by handing over temporary responsibility for their child).

Danger gets through your filter system to a remarkable extent. A friend of mine sleeping happily on a flight on a small propeller driven plane woke up suddenly and could not work out why until he realised that, there was no sound of an engine. It was the silence that had created the threat that got through his RAS. Happily the pilot was able to land the plane without

44

mishap and my friend lived to tell the harrowing tale.

If you bought a new car recently, it is likely that you will remember that suddenly, after collecting it, you noticed loads of that make (and probably colour) of car on the road – they had always been there but, once you invested a significant amount of your money in one, your subconscious sought to give you reassurance (that you made a wise investment) by filtering through to you the recognition that lots of other people were of a like mind.

For now, it is vital to appreciate how the function of your RAS limits what you see and hear and how you can prime your RAS to make you aware of information around you that will help you achieve your goals.

When you set yourself goals, whether at home or at work, you are effectively priming your RAS with the message 'information that will help me achieve ... will be valuable – so let me be aware of it'. You are at the same time sending the message 'information that will help me achieve MORE than ... will NOT be valuable – so DO NOT MAKE ME AWARE OF IT'.

In the corporate sector this concept can have an astonishing effect on sales. Some years ago I was helping the board of directors of a computer company and the sales director's challenge was that he believed the company could sell 15 (huge and vastly expensive) computers that year but his sales managers could not see sales higher than seven in a year. After he explained this concept to his team they raised their target to 30 and within 12 months managed to sell 28. Interestingly, and in my view shockingly, they were told they had failed as their target had been 30. The fact that they had nearly doubled the performance anticipated by their sales director was completely overlooked.

Until now it is possible that you may have unwittingly been limiting your successes by setting your goals at a 'realistic' level – based perhaps on what you already know 'how to' achieve – rather than aiming for your ideal.

When you set goals, in the way I am recommending, you are not guaranteeing success and you do need to recognise that sometimes it will take a while for your RAS to find you the resources and answers you need. I suggest you experiment with the function of your RAS, and discover how it can help you on simple things, in order to gain the confidence to start to stretch your goals in areas of your life that are more significant for you. (If you decide on your next car journey that you want to count how many red cars you pass that have a number 4 in their numberplate, I bet you will be astonished how they will catch your eye, without your even scanning for them.)

I will expand later in the book on the benefits of ensuring that the goals you set are at the limit of your inner self-belief in what you can achieve.

I will also address the need to develop resilience if it takes longer to achieve your goals than you had hoped.

Assimilated beliefs

Some people are irritated when they're told "you can do it if you put your mind to it". This only goes to suggest that they do not understand how their mind works.

All your life you have been filling your mind with a mass of information that allows you to carry on your daily life, without necessarily needing to think too much about what to do, or how to do it – it just flows naturally.

Regrettably some of the information you have assimilated continues to limit you in terms of what you achieve, and indeed what you aspire to achieve.

If in your childhood, a teacher, a parent, or an authority of some kind expressed an opinion (positive or negative) about your potential in a particular area, the chances are that you may well have believed them. Unrecognised by you that belief is likely to remain lodged in your subconscious and (if it was negative) may be limiting your choices to this day.

In the world of computer programming there has long been a saying that if you put garbage in you will get garbage out (known as the GIGO principle). In terms of your mental computer, if you have regrettably allowed garbage in, in the past, that stored garbage may well be influencing you still when you seek to make choices today.

I will expand on this theme later, but it is really important to recognise firstly that the memories you have stored are based both on the perceptions you had and on the emotions you felt in the past, and secondly, as you saw at the beginning of this chapter, that your perceptions may have had little to do with reality or 'the truth'.

Being committed to your *ideal* goals

At the highest level of competition being fully committed to your goal is essential.

Helping people to set, and be fully committed to, ambitious goals at the ideal level is what every coach aspires to, yet few have the means to help the client check the suitability of the goal, or to verify whether there is any subconscious resistance.

The significance of this to you sports stars is huge. Most people, even sports stars at Olympic level, set goals that are within, rather than at the top edge of, their inner beliefs about what they could have, or achieve.

Using my approach to tap into your subconscious/inner self-belief will allow a coach to get in touch with your real desires and needs. That is a great first step to helping you to fulfil your potential.

The next step is to check whether setting this higher aspiration has triggered any doubts or concerns in your subconscious and how much resistance is lurking at the back of your mind that is inhibiting your success.

There is often a great deal of this subconscious sabotage, and I have even seen clients with an initial resistance level of 100% to the achievement of their 'ideal' goal.

In the next chapter, 'Clearing the track', I will be describing the four elements of our conditioning that combine to generate this resistance and hold all of us back from using more of our potential.

Actions steps for you to take:

I encourage you to look at your goals and see if you can stretch them to be more ideal and exciting for you.

Then get the help you need to see if your goals are now stretched to the limits of your inner belief about what you see as possible for you.

Clearing the track

The key points:

Your capacity to see options and opportunities is often restricted by your conditioning (especially your beliefs).

When you are 'stuck', or not progressing, the root cause will almost certainly be found in one or more of a combination of four elements.

Spotting your own 'Creative Avoidance' will alert you to the presence of either a counterproductive attitude or a sense of coercion.

Most coaches work in a way that does not access the unconscious beliefs, attitudes, fears, or expectations of their clients.

To ensure you are fully committed to your optimum success, and are free of subconscious sabotage, you need a coach who has been trained to work at the level of your unconscious thoughts and beliefs.

If you already do a lot of mental preparation or psychological training with your coach you may think you do not need to read this chapter – and that is fine by me provided you understand *why* mental simulation and 'mind games' actually work.

Unless you understand the science behind what I call 'mind games' you are unlikely to use them with 100% commitment and application.

Without that level of application you may let yourself down when the pressure is really on, perhaps in an Olympic final when you have one last throw, or jump, to get your medal, perhaps when you have an eight foot putt on the 18th green to win a golf match.

This chapter will clarify for you the elements that contribute to the subconscious sabotage that tends to lurk in the back of your mind – especially when you set yourself a really ambitious target.

Your conditioning - the 'C' of the 'ABC' model

When I suggest that what restricts your progress is a blend of these four elements - your beliefs, expectations, habits, and attitudes - it may sound as if they would be easy for you to change.

However, as they are tucked away in your subconscious, and have a great deal to do with how you behave in an instinctive way, it is not always easy to identify the ones that need changing as opposed to the ones that are helping you.

Some of the elements combine to trigger a counterproductive trait, 'Creative Avoidance', that clients tell me is one of the most significant concepts they have gained from my workshops.

Before exploring the four elements in turn, and explaining this key trait, I want to give you a simple model of how you make decisions.

Making choices – decision making

Research by Dr Wilder Penfield, the pioneering neurosurgeon, has demonstrated that we have a memory of all our past experiences (or at least our perception of them) stored in our brain and these form the basis of many of our beliefs, expectations, and attitudes, thereby influencing unduly the choices we make about our future.

You may not be aware that you make choices, for the immediate or more distant future, by using a potentially flawed decision making process.

When faced by a range of options, you cast your mind back to see whether you have a memory of something similar to any of the options under consideration.

Seemingly relevant experiences are brought forward, from your memory, to a part of the brain called the 'Common Integrative Area' (or CIA for short). It is this part of your brain which leads you to function in line with your current belief system – even though your beliefs may be based on limited or false perceptions.

When you think about setting a new goal your CIA scans for similar experiences in your past, and attitudes and expectations, which have been lurking at a subconscious level, will be triggered.

Unfortunately your ability to make constructive decisions is often restricted by past experiences that left a stressful or unhappy memory. Provided, on the other hand, a past experience was pleasant, or successful, this is likely to trigger a memory which generates positive attitudes and expectations which will help you to choose, and pursue, the new goal with real commitment.

The following chart simply illustrates how your response is likely to vary, depending on your recollection of past events.

The Barometer of Choice

	RESULT	Free choice
	STATE OF MIND	Positive
	ATTITUDE	Confident
	RECALL	Joyful
	MEMORY	Happy
Stressful	**EVENT**	**Pleasant**
Traumatic	MEMORY	
Painful	RECALL	
Apprehensive	ATTITUDE	
Negative	STATE OF MIND	
Limited choice	RESULT	

When seeing an opportunity, perhaps to join some friends on an outing, to enter a challenging competition, or to branch out on your own in a new venture, you instantly and automatically dip into your memory, to see if you have had a similar experience before and consider how likely it is that you will enjoy the suggested option. Based on the feedback you get from your memory you are then likely to make your decision whether to go for it or not.

I suggested to you earlier in the book that there are all sorts of reasons why we only see part of the 'truth'. Unfortunately it is our part 'truth', rather than the full 'truth', that we store in our subconscious memory.

We all tend to make spontaneous decisions based on our memory of past experiences, and our incomplete perception/memory, rather than on our present strengths and potential.

I have no doubt that one of the reasons so many athletes set aspirations below their potential is because of memories, and perceptions, lodged in their subconscious, which have no relevance to them or their performance today.

I now want to look in turn at the significance and relevance of each of the four elements of your conditioning that can hold you back from greater success.

Beliefs

We have already seen how beliefs can limit what opportunities we see, affect how we look at things, and even blind us to reality.

Disappointing outcomes in the past, perhaps at school, or when competing in some sport, may have led to you develop self-limiting beliefs which are based on partial and/or distorted perceptions of your earlier experiences.

Something really important for you to recognise is that other beliefs, about what is or is not possible for you, will have been accumulated over time from the opinions of others that you have sanctioned.

Throughout your life your teachers, parents, older siblings, and other 'experts' will have given you their opinion of your ability in everything from academic subjects, to your sporting talent and prospects, your musical prowess, or your dress sense.

When you were young it is quite likely that you accepted (sanctioned) these opinions without question, which is understandable, and will have done you no harm, provided the opinion given to you was encouraging, appealing or aspirational.

If, on the other hand, as is sadly so often the case, the opinion was a negative one, such as "you'll never be able to...", "no-one has ever ...", "don't be so stupid", "who are you to think you could ...", and if these limiting views were sanctioned by you, then regrettably a counterproductive belief probably started to build in your subconscious which, if not reversed, may continue to limit you from even attempting things which may well be within your scope.

The world of sport and athletics offer many examples of experts who got it wrong.

Guin Batten was told that she was 'too small' to be in the GB rowing squad, in spite of being top of the ERG machine results. She went on to prove herself, at world level, as a single sculler, and was then brought back into the quadruple scull GB boat which won the Olympic silver medal in 2000.

Very interestingly Boris Becker, when asked how he had managed to win the Wimbledon men's singles tennis title at the age of 17, replied that luckily for him no-one had told him he was too young to do so – no-one imagined that he could think that he could win it at that age (or they would probably 'sagely' have told him not to be so stupid). He saw no reason why he could not simply play one game at a time and by doing so famously went on to win the final.

For years the medical world 'knew' it was physically impossible for man to run a mile in under four minutes. This belief delayed the breaking of that barrier until Roger Bannister achieved his goal of proving the medical experts wrong in 1954 and opened the floodgates to many other athletes who broke the barrier within the next 12 months.

Had their technique suddenly improved? No – their belief in whether or not it was humanly possible had been changed.

I will return to the fact that, as individuals, teams and organisations, we tend to perform in a way that matches our long held beliefs rather than fulfilling our potential.

For now, I urge you to be careful about the opinions of others that you accept and sanction for yourself.

One of the great teachers I have been lucky enough to meet in my life was Gordon Stokes who trained me to teach kinesiology. He grew up in America and as a child did not realise that his eyesight was not brilliant.

When at school, he struggled to see what was written on the blackboard. In his particular school the less able boys were sent towards the back of the class and, because his work suffered through not being able to read what was written on the blackboard, he progressively moved further and further away from the blackboard, was less and less able to read it, and ended up in the back row of the class being told he was 'thick and stupid' − a belief shared, and acted upon, by all of his teachers.

In that era, in America, some form of national service was obligatory and Gordon, curiously perhaps given that he lived deep in the middle of the country and far from the sea, chose to go into the Navy. He had a long train journey from his home to the coast, where the naval college was based, during which, he once explained to me, he firstly reflected that he thought he was actually quite bright, and secondly that there would be no-one at the naval college who knew he was 'thick and stupid'.

As part of the medical assessment at the start of his training his need for spectacles became apparent. Once suitably equipped he was able to read and understand what was written on the board and that, combined with hard work and the firmly held belief that he was bright, enabled him to pass out top of his intake at the end of the training.

He was lucky that he had the self-belief to challenge the frequently delivered verdict of his schoolmasters. Most of us struggle to identify the beliefs that are holding us back.

I recommend you to find a suitably qualified coach who can help you to check on the beliefs you hold about yourself, and your aspirations, and see whether these are limited by events or opinions sanctioned in your past – in which case you would do well to adjust them.

Expectations

Your expectations, as highlighted by the 'Barometer of Choice' at the start of this chapter, are clearly based on your memory of previous experiences or on others' descriptions of their experiences. They can equally flow from what you have read or heard recently about the environment you are living in or visiting. They can also be based on your perception of yourself as accumulated from past experiences.

If they are negative expectations they may well be unjustified, yet they will often influence your choices or your ability to enjoy your day (as explained in the earlier section on the cognitive dissonance concept and the 'sure enough' principle).

For example, the perception/belief 'I am a dreadful cook' deters many people from inviting friends around to dinner, because of the expectation that they will ruin the meal and the evening will be a disaster. Equally the commonly held perception 'I'm no good at speaking in public' has put many people off from proposing the toast at the wedding of a friend or relation, because they expect to feel nervous, speak badly, and look foolish.

A very competent golfer, when he was captain of his golf club, amazed me when he said, "I always struggle on the first few holes and then settle into my game". I explained that this belief was programming him to play down to the low level of his expectation, and told him that what he needed to do, if he wanted to play to his potential, was to stop programming himself to struggle on the early holes and to build an expectation of getting off to a better start. Happily, the other day he assured me he now regularly gets a par on each of the early holes and that gets him off to a great start in his games.

Later, after I have elaborated on how these beliefs/perceptions build up and how you can change them to give yourself more options, I hope you will understand more about the extent to which your expectations come from what you tell yourself about yourself.

To understand how 'mind games' will help you (if used correctly) you will need to understand the significance of the fact that your beliefs and expectations have contributed to your existing, multifaceted, self-image, which is your subconscious picture of yourself that is driving your behaviour.

I will be expanding on this at length in the 'Getting in the zone' chapter. For now, I hope you can accept that, for any activity, your subconscious self-image 'knows' how much you enjoy it, how good you think you are at it, and the extent to which you look forward to it.

Appropriately used, 'mind games' will enable you to adjust your beliefs and expectations, develop a new self-image in line with your aspirations, and thereby underpin your progress.

Habits

Habitual behaviour can obviously have invaluable advantages. Once you have performed a task, or a skill, enough times – such as tying your shoe laces, or changing gear in a car – you no longer need to think how to do it, or what to do next. You are able to perform it automatically, as if it were on autopilot, while thinking of, or indeed doing, one or more other actions at the same time.

Regrettably this can lead to you continuing to perform a task in your habitual way long after more convenient, or economical, alternatives have been available.

One example of this I heard was that airlines flying from Seattle to London used to refuel either in Chicago or in New York. This route became so established in their minds that when planes became capable of reaching London without refuelling, pilots continued flying over Chicago and New York, en route to London, not recognising for some time that a quicker and cheaper route was available by flying more directly.

To take some sporting examples: when high jumpers were in the habit of using the 'Western Roll', I well remember reading that medical experts, and sports coaches, were advising athletes not to try and emulate Fosbury's 'flop' style. Hundreds of athletes tried it immediately and many set personal best heights, including David Hemery when he did the decathlon a year after his hurdling triumph in Mexico. Today, it is still recognised as the most successful approach.

Similarly, ski jumpers, for many years, jumped with their skis together before someone made the breakthrough by obtaining greater lift, and thereby jumping further, by spreading their skis in a V shape.

I have frequently heard "We have always done it this way" in businesses (in the board room as well as on the shop floor) as justification for continuing with an outdated or costly process.

Sometimes we become very attached to 'our way of doing things'. Being expected to change a habit is likely to trigger some resistance, until we recognise the benefits of the new approach and until we have learnt a comfortable way to acquire the new habit.

A good while ago I was intrigued to work with a sales team in a life insurance company who had always been used to making handwritten notes at their meetings with prospective clients. They were appalled when their boss decreed that from now on, when with a prospect, they would be required to fill in forms on a laptop instead (thereby saving the considerable time it took to transcribe their notes on returning to the office).

In the sports world, serious competitors work hard to develop and improve their technique. They are keen to acquire the habit of performing at a consistently skilful level. In the chapter on 'mind games', I will be describing and illustrating how you can use your brain like a simulator, to the point where you will do better to perform free-flowingly, in an automatic rather than consciously thought out way, relying on your subconsciously embedded technique to instinctively produce the performance you are seeking.

There is an easy and natural way to assimilate new habits and, later, I will be introducing you to that comfortable change process and looking at some of the other reasons why people resist change.

Attitudes

I mentioned earlier that I would introduce you to the concept of 'creative avoidance' that has been greatly appreciated by many of my clients and students in the past.

I once sent a list of maybe 30 concepts that I cover in my workshops to 200 or so former participants and asked them to indicate those concepts that they had found especially helpful or life-changing.

I was really interested that 'creative avoidance' was the only concept that *everyone* replying to my survey told me had been particularly significant for them. I therefore hope it will also be eye-opening for you.

It seems that all of us have things that we regularly put off doing. It might be mowing the lawn, doing homework, ironing, or even something much less time-consuming.

Before you can change that particular bad habit, should you have it, you probably need an understanding of what is causing you to put off doing things that may be quite urgent or important.

You might want to pause for a moment and list some things that *you* 'creatively avoid' doing...

I'm going to suggest to you that when you look at your list there are two likely reasons that typically cause you to put off doing these things. One is that you are telling yourself that you "have to" do it (or "must" do it, "ought to" do it, "have got to do it", "should" do it etc.) – all examples of coercive language – the other reason is likely to be that you have a negative attitude about the task.

When someone first explained this idea to me I understood a situation that I regularly used to find myself in.

Before I go on holiday I like everything to be up to date and to have nothing outstanding on my desk.

For years, as holiday time got closer, there would always be a pile of non-urgent letters I needed to reply to. Instead of replying to each of them as they arrived I had found something 'more important', or perhaps 'more appealing', to do instead.

Once I had decided to tackle the pile of correspondence, I not only enjoyed the process of writing the needed letters, but discovered that each one could be completed in a comparatively short space of time. I realised that I had, from somewhere, acquired an attitude about writing letters. It did not take me long to identify the origins of that particular attitude.

Looking back at my childhood, I am in no doubt that my attitude started with the chore of writing immaculate 'thank-you' letters at Christmas. I was fortunate to be blessed with many godparents, as well as my grandparents and a number of aunts and uncles, who generously sent me gifts. My parents expected my 'thank-you' letters to be not only spelt correctly but without any alterations or grammatical errors. Each letter would probably need writing at least twice before my parents considered it acceptable.

Reflecting on that now, and on the pleasure I have gained from the spontaneous and sometimes gloriously mis-spelt offerings from my own nephews, nieces and godchildren, I think it's a great shame that mine needed to be so perfect. I can also quite understand that it left me with a dread of the prospect of writing letters, and a habit of 'creative avoidance', that lasted well into my 30s.

So, quite simply, I am suggesting your attitudes have been accumulated over time. Based on your enjoyment, or otherwise, of previous experiences, they give you enthusiasm for some activities and resistance to others.

Most, if not all, of us naturally back away from, or try to avoid, doing things that we have not enjoyed in the past and will actively volunteer for things we expect to get pleasure or satisfaction from.

I will go into greater depth later, on the fact that people can only be genuinely committed to a goal when they believe they can achieve it. Doubts, triggered by past failures or disappointments, are likely to demotivate us and I will suggest later how you can boost your confidence, belief, and self-esteem (preferably with expert help) so as to overcome any possible subconscious sabotage that may be triggered by your memories of past events.

You may have heard yourself, or others, referred to as having 'positive' or 'negative' attitudes. In reality, attitudes are neither positive nor negative until associated with a goal or task, when they will then incline us towards, or away from, the activity in question.

There are many attitudes in the workplace, in relationships, and in sport, about the abilities of each sex.

In the early days, when I watched Wimbledon tennis on TV, commentators explained that the comparatively gentle serves delivered by ladies were the result of the limitations imposed by their physical make-up.

To watch the serves powered down by the ladies of today I can only conclude the commentators' explanation was nonsense – but perhaps the players of yesteryear believed that biological view?

A shockingly recent business example of an attitude, is that of a good friend of mine who, while attending a board meeting of a nationally respected business, of which she was a director, put forward a proposal that was warmly greeted and accepted. She happened to see the minutes of the meeting a few days later and was shocked to discover that her idea had been attributed to the male CEO.

I have often been shown a cartoon of a meeting in a boardroom with just one lady in attendance. The caption reads "That is an excellent idea Miss Triggs, perhaps one of the men here would like to make it". Until I heard my friend's story I had always thought this cartoon an exaggeration – now I think of her whenever I see it.

Before reading the next section, I invite you to look at the list of things that you have, until now, 'creatively avoided' and see whether you can identify any attitudes that may be involved and be causing the problem – if you can, you may want to change them (and the 'mind games' chapter will help you do that).

I now want to expand on the careless coercive phrases people so often use that are the second possible trigger of 'creative avoidance'.

Modal operators of necessity

This is a concept from Neuro Linguistic Programming (NLP). I studied this very effective technique many years ago and discovered how you can use physical and verbal 'triggers' to improve your chances of delivering your best performance.

Within that extensive training was an important section that explained why you are better off excluding words and phrases like "I have to", "I must", "I've got to", "I should", and "I ought to", known as 'Modal operators of necessity', from your vocabulary.

Why? Because they are all heard (by your subconscious) as being 'coercive' and interestingly they are likely to trigger resistance to whatever you are referring to – even if the activity appeals to you.

The healthier your self-esteem is, the more likely you are to resist coercive pressure. Human beings do not like people trying to push them around and tend instinctively to push back against the pusher.

I want you to understand that, very interestingly, your subconscious responds to your own coercive words by triggering the same response. If it considers that you are pushing yourself around it will therefore resist.

Because your subconscious also interprets your own coercive words as meaning that you would rather be doing something else, it therefore steers you in that alternative and preferable direction, even to the point that you may try to get out of doing things that you would expect to find enjoyable ('creative avoidance' at its craziest).

Now that you are aware of its significance, and detrimental impact, I think you will be astonished at the amount of coercive language you will hear yourself using. It may be reassuring to hear that others around you also use it extensively, but I recommend that from now on you recognise how much in your life can be seen as a free choice.

All you need to do to reduce the risk of sabotaging your success and enjoyment by careless use of 'Modal operators of necessity', is adjust your use of language to eliminate coercive words and phrases.

In the chapter on effective 'mind games' I will give you some advice on self-talk.

For now, in this context, when you hear yourself using coercive language on yourself I recommend you change the "have to/must/got to/ought to" language to phrases such as "I want to", or sometimes "I need to" which I find generates some urgency without being coercive.

Freedom of choice

Once you accept that your 'creative avoidance' is usually triggered by coercive language, and/or a negative attitude caused by unpleasant memories, it is a really useful 'alert' to be aware of. I suggest you prime your RAS to alert you to your 'creative avoidance' in case there is something that urgently needs to be done.

From now on, whenever you find yourself putting something off, ask yourself whether you are using coercive language or whether perhaps you have an attitude it would pay you to adjust.

With this understanding you can then ensure that you live your life enjoying the freedom to do whatever you aspire to, rather than seeking freedom from less

66

attractive options, and you can review your habitual behaviour, to check that it is not holding you back from new levels of success.

Accountability

Once you recognise the abundant choice of behaviours open to you, you can healthily start to take more conscious control of your choices – provided you are prepared to accept the consequences of those decisions.

With the recognition of your freedom of choice comes an increased realisation that the responsibility for how your life will be in the future is within your own grasp, perhaps to a far greater degree than you have previously acknowledged.

Removing subconscious sabotage

I hope this realisation becomes more exciting for you when you link it to these psychological concepts (especially those concerning your self-belief and self-image), and to the availability of this new coaching approach to unleash your potential.

We have had a long look at your conditioning, the 'C' from the 'ABC' model, and the four elements that tend to trigger resistance to your achieving your goals. When I am coaching clients they are often astonished that they can have 100% commitment to a newly identified goal (that they are both consciously and subconsciously happy with) and yet have a significant level of resistance to it.

On more than one occasion I've seen 100% resistance in clients where the new goal was seen to be more than they thought they deserved, or more than they had ever thought of achieving.

I suspect you can imagine how much their confidence is enhanced when we reach the point that they have 100% commitment, to a goal that is at the upper edge of their inner self-belief, and when I have reduced their resistance level to 0%.

In the next chapter of the book 'Getting in the zone' we will be looking at the significance of all the aspects of your self-concept, the 'D' of the 'ABC of Success' model, which is the key to understanding why things are currently as they are for you, and what you will be able to do to improve them.

Actions steps for you to take:

Think carefully before accepting the opinion of others.

Notice yourself demonstrating 'creative avoidance' and check for any unhelpful attitudes you need to change.

Eliminate coercive language and thereby reduce the risk of triggering 'creative avoidance' – in yourself or in others.

Get your coach to check that you do not have any subconscious restraints holding you back from achieving your ambitions.

Getting in the zone

The key points:

You have accumulated thoughts about yourself with your self-talk throughout your life.

These have established a multifaceted self-image.

You have a comfort zone around each element of your self-image and are at your free-flowing best when within it.

When out of your comfort zone you will instinctively seek to return to it as soon as possible.

Your free-flowing performance will be a reflection of your self-image – so if you want a sustainable and progressive change in your performance, you need to change your self-image and its corresponding comfort zone (preferably with an instinctive and comfortable process).

As your performance continues to improve, you need your coach to check whether your subconscious self-efficacy has increased – and stretch your goal, if appropriate.

The impact of the self-concept

Something really significant I want you to appreciate is that your free-flowing behaviour or performance is, and always will be, a reflection of your subconscious self-image.

That being the case, it follows that the most natural way to change your behaviour, or performance level, is to adjust your self-image. It also follows that if you try and improve your performance, without changing your self-image, it will be very much harder, if not impossible, for you to achieve consistent levels of success.

It is therefore really important, if you want to improve your performance, that you understand how your self-image gets built, and what you can do to change it with a process that is not only instinctive, but is also comfortable (and, at the same time, ensures that your progress is sustainable).

Look at this variation of the 'ABC of Success' model.

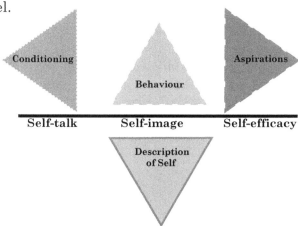

The upper level, Aspirations, Behaviour, and Conditioning, is the level at which most coaches operate.

The elements below the horizontal line, rather as

with an iceberg, reveal what is usually out of sight and yet is the most important part to be aware of – your self-talk, your self-image, and your self-efficacy – the components of your 'Description of yourself' – the D in the 'ABC' model.

I want you to repeat my mantra that "to get to A from B you need to work on C & D".

The three elements of your description of yourself keep you acting like you, aspiring for things that you feel you deserve, and staying in your comfort zone.

I have described how your beliefs, expectations, habits and attitudes may be the cause of your being stuck in a rut, or being unable to move forward to use more of your potential.

Understanding about the impact of your many comfort zones will complete the picture of what will hold you back (unless you know how to overcome these natural restraints).

Until now, when wanting to improve on your own personal or sporting performance, it is probable that you will have been focused on that performance rather than on the barriers to your progress and other underlying issues.

In your life, or your career, you may have seen temporary changes, or improvements in performance, before standards have dropped back to their previous level. New Year's resolutions are a classic example of this.

The key to understanding this trend, and reversing it, is to appreciate the link between your performance and your self-image. Your subconscious has a multifaceted picture of you, and of how well you typically perform your routine tasks and hobbies.

For sanity, your subconscious will keep your performance in line with your expectations. In other words it will ensure that you act 'like you', even though that standard of performance may be well below your potential.

That is why, when people start to make progress towards a new performance level, the rate of improvement so often slows down, or grinds to a halt, and before long they steadily revert back to their 'usual' performance.

If you want sustainable improvements the best way is to change your self-image first, thereby adjusting your comfort zone, and then let the improvements gradually and incrementally follow.

Comfort zones

Your self-image is the product of your self-talk. You no doubt describe yourself to others in terms of "I am really quick out of the blocks", "My golf handicap is stuck at ...", "I can see myself ....", "I am shy/confident", "I am a good driver", "I can't cook to save my life", "I like ...", and these statements about yourself are accepted and collated by your subconscious.

When you were young, you probably sanctioned the opinions expressed about you by your parents, teachers, or anyone else you saw as authorities, and also maybe by an elder sibling, or a friend. They probably told you what you did well, and sadly (if you believed them) what they thought you were never going to be any good at.

The act of sanctioning the opinion of another is akin to saying "Yes, I am like that, you are right". By accepting others' opinions, and by expressing your own, you establish and reinforce your self-image and thus increasingly create the boundaries within which you are likely to perform.

These boundaries are called your comfort zones. They represent a margin, on either side of your self-image, in every sphere, within which you are comfortable and able to perform in a free-flowing way. Once you are taken outside your comfort zone, you instinctively do your best to get back to 'being like me', as soon as possible.

It is really important to recognise that you will have a comfort zone around every facet of your self-image.

If someone is in sales, and 'sees' themselves as usually selling ten items a month, then their comfort zone might be between eight and 12 items a month. After a bad month, if they sold just six items, it would perhaps not surprise you to hear that they would be quite likely to pull out all the stops and sell 12 or 14 the next month.

Crazy as it might seem to you though, if that salesperson has a really good month and sells more than 12 they are likely to adjust, at a subconscious level, for the mistake of doing 'too well for them' and sell very few the next month.

Unless their targets are adjusted, most sales teams and individuals will find that, by the end of the year, their sales are in line with their original expectations/self-image. How much better might their performance be if, after every good month, they raised their expectations to sell that many every month?

Remember that your performance will be in line with your self-image that has been built up by your self-talk.

Very few people seem to know this and all day long I hear counterproductive self-talk being used that is programming the user to underachieve.

In particular, listening to friends on the golf course gives me an endless stream of examples of the concept.

"Why do I always do that?" an opponent asked me recently after mis-hitting an iron shot, that he had hoped would land on the green, but instead had gone well wide.

I could have answered that the reason was quite simply that he was telling his subconscious to ensure he did it every time – but I decided it was not the occasion to do so.

Remember the example I gave you of the self-destructive captain of his golf club who told me "I always struggle on the first few holes and then settle into my game"?

In much healthier contrast, a different golf opponent on a different course, playing off a handicap of about 18, told me as we stood on the first tee "I've got used to getting par on the first two holes" (better than his handicap would suggest was likely). He actually got a par and a birdie that day.

These are all examples of how our self-talk builds up our self-image and how our subconscious then does its best to get us to perform 'like us'.

Individuals, teams, and organisations all self-regulate in line with their self-images.

The manager of a newly-built paint plant once told me that they had reached their planned production level within a few months of starting up. Everyone had been well pleased with the performance, the plant was clean, and morale was great.

After being introduced to these concepts, the managers and supervisors realised that the plant had settled into a comfort zone. They raised their sights, shared their vision with the staff, and within a short time productivity had risen by an astonishing 30%, to a volume way higher than the plant had been designed for.

The inevitability of unexpected meetings, or events, means that you will not always be able to be sure to be in your comfort zone.

I am sure you are familiar with signs that you are out of your comfort zone – you may feel physically tense, you may sense a tightening in your chest from anxiety, you may not speak confidently etc. From now on, I expect you will also recognise when you instinctively take steps to get back into feeling comfortable at the earliest opportunity.

Becoming aware of when you are out of your comfort zone can at times be extremely valuable. There may well be occasions when you are in a dangerous situation and your subconscious will do its best to alert you to the problem by making you feel uncomfortable.

Many years ago, I wanted to thank some decorators for doing a good and timely job for me and suggested we went to a local London pub for a drink. I was new to the area and did not realise that the pub I had chosen was known to be the haunt of the local villains. We had only been in the pub a few seconds before I was feeling thoroughly out of place, and it felt as if the hairs were standing up on the back of my neck.

I have seldom downed a pint quicker, and I am somewhat embarrassed to admit that I got away from the pub as fast as possible, leaving my bemused painters happily settling down to their drinks and crisps.

A more curious example occurred in the early 1970s when I went to one of my favourite restaurants in London. As I sat down at a table I felt really uneasy. I looked around but could see nothing that set my alarm bells ringing, nor was there anyone in the restaurant that I was unhappy to see there.

I was really intrigued when I spotted the cause of my discomfort – the chicken wire had been removed from the inside of the windows.

For this story to make sense you need to know that for some months in the 1970s, the IRA had been inclined to throw bombs through the windows of London restaurants and pubs, and we had all got used to seeing chicken wire protecting the windows in any venue we went into.

It amazed me that my subconscious had picked up that something was wrong (the protection had gone), and I therefore felt unsafe, even though the restaurant now looked 'normal'.

Adjusting comfort zones

When you think about setting new goals, do you aim for the best possible picture and trust that you have the potential to achieve it?

Do you "Go for Gold" or "Go for Bronze" if you are an Olympian?

Perhaps you set 'realistic' targets, or goals based on your current comfort zones and expectations?

I have encouraged you to set ideal goals, without necessarily knowing *how* to get there. What matters is that you can 'see yourself' doing it - whatever the 'it' might be.

Where 'it' would currently be outside your comfort zone you will either need to adjust your comfort zone, or change your self-image (and thereby your comfort zone), to be able to perform free-flowingly at the new level.

You might want a broad comfort zone when it comes to the sort of restaurants and cafés you feel comfortable eating in, you might want a very narrow comfort zone to keep your sporting, or professional, achievements at a high level.

Watching the Rugby World Cup in 2015, I was struck by the consistency of the penalty takers. They didn't just succeed with their kicks – more often than not they bisected the posts with an astonishing display of accuracy.

This will be in part the result of developing the necessary skills and then setting themselves the goal of maintaining that very precise standard. It will also be, in part, the result of having a very narrow comfort zone around that aspect of their self-image, and also doubtless, in part, the result of employing the 'mind games' I will be describing later.

Comfort zones impact sporting performance

I want to return to the suggestion that when you are out of your comfort zone your subconscious will get creative to get you back 'where you belong'. This is really significant for you to understand if you are competing in any sport.

If you are a golfer, my next example is likely to ring many bells for you.

Let us suppose you have a handicap of 18. If, after the first nine holes, you see that your score is 15 over par (rather than nine over par if you were playing to your handicap/'like you'), it is quite likely that you will play the last nine holes in three or four over par, bringing your final score in line with your self-image/comfort zone for that course.

Conversely, if you discover that you have been playing 'too well for you' on the front nine, your subconscious is likely to correct for that mistake and again bring your score more in line with your handicap by the end of the back nine (unless you are very careful to talk yourself into maintaining that 'higher than usual' level of play).

If you are a golfer, aspiring athlete, or ambitious sports star, you need to know how to adjust your self-talk and your self-image if your performance is to reach an elite, or more successful, level.

I believe one of the saddest sporting examples of someone doing 'too well for them' was the 1993 Wimbledon ladies' tennis final between Steffi Graf and Jana Novotna. Steffi Graf was the world number one player at the time and Novotna was no doubt encouraged that Graf only won the first set on a tie-break.

Astonishingly, Novotna then proceeded to break Graf's service frequently, while holding her own, and won the second set by six games to one. She then established a lead of four games to one in the third set.

Serving at 40/30 she was one point away from leading the final set by five games to one. Had she won the next point she would have won nine of the last 11 games. However, she served a double fault and went on to lose her service. Famously, she never won another game in the match, losing the final set by four games to six.

My guess is that Novotna went on court believing she could win. I think she could see herself holding up the trophy. I do not believe she could imagine herself thrashing the world number one. I suspect that the thought of winning both of the last two sets by six games to one took her way out of her comfort zone.

I am convinced that her subconscious started correcting for the fact that she was doing 'too well for her', by getting her to serve many more double faults and repeatedly lose her service. Graf (who afterwards confirmed that "I'd kind of lost it ... I didn't give up hope but didn't have a very positive feeling") grew in confidence with each game she won, and the rest is history.

It is really important that you understand the significance of how you talk to yourself, especially when things are not going as you would like, and in the next section I will start to look at how this impacts your performance.

Modal operators of possibility

In NLP you learn not only about the 'Modal operators of necessity' but also 'Modal operators of possibility'. The implication of the latter is that when you tell yourself you cannot do something, this 'careless talk' sends messages to the brain that reduces your self-efficacy and generates counterproductive behaviour.

What is important for you to remember is that your subconscious will take literally what you say. It does not recognise a careless, throw-away line. It believes what you tell it and then acts accordingly. So please, from now on, prime your RAS to hear any careless self-talk you use and reverse it before any damage is done.

In the case of 'Modal operators of possibility', examples of the language to avoid would be: "I can't", "we'll never do it", "I'm no good at this", "there's no way", "I've had it now", "it's hopeless".

Hearing such language, even in an area where you have the talent to succeed, your subconscious would rather you failed but looked sane, than succeeded and looked crazy.

The important point to grasp is that if you want to use your potential, since you will tend to perform in line with your perceptions and descriptions of your abilities, you need to take great care to use 'Modal operators of possibility'.

Phrases like "we'll find a way to ...", "it must be possible", "I haven't *yet* found ...", or "I'll get there" will help you to keep going in pursuit of what you are looking to find, or achieve.

Are you one of those people who is often unable to find something that turns out to be 'under your nose', or is in your handbag all the time? I referred to this problem in the first chapter and a great example, that I have often seen, shows how powerful this simple idea can be.

It occurs, for instance, when someone – usually a lady, 'cannot find their keys in their handbag'. I have watched countless people rummage in their (often quite small) bag for a shiny-looking, noisy-sounding, sharp-feeling, cold-feeling bunch of keys. They curiously are usually not even looking in the bag but staring into space somewhere as they protest "I cannot find my keys".

A miracle occurs every time they follow my request to 1) take their hand out of their bag, 2) look me in the eye and repeat after me, "I am going to put my hand in my bag and take my keys out", 3) find their keys in their bag.

It has never yet failed (provided the keys were in the bag in the first place). How interesting it is to note that when in "I can't …" mode they often do not even LOOK for their keys (rather just stare into space) − perhaps their subconscious is creatively trying to make it harder for them, in order to reduce the risk of them looking foolish by finding what they are saying they cannot?

This simple concept of 'Modal operators of possibility' seems to be an eye-opener for most people and one that they see as really important to understand. Some years ago, I was asked to give a talk at Price Waterhouse Coopers' London headquarters on 'self-efficacy in the workplace'. At the start of my talk, as a means of grabbing the audience's attention, I invited people who had trouble finding their keys in their handbag to raise their hands (so that I could see how many would be interested in hearing how to overcome that problem). Many hands were raised, I promised to help them address that issue, and I launched into my talk with a highly attentive audience.

At the end of my talk, the question and answer session that followed kept to the corporate application of self-efficacy, and, when the chairman announced that he was closing the meeting, there were howls of protest from ladies demanding to know how to find their keys.

Happily for them I was given a few extra minutes to let them in on the secret. Some ladies told me afterwards that it was by far the most important bit of the evening for them and now they could see many practical applications of 'Modal operators of possibility'.

Self-esteem

A key element of your self-efficacy is your self-esteem. Both are task specific, or as one executive put it to me, contextual.

Self-esteem can be very fragile. I was astonished to discover, from a survey of a large group of MDs who had attended my workshops, that learning how to develop their self-esteem and confidence was by far the most important concept they had learnt.

The MDs' self-esteem was fragile because their prominent roles and responsibilities added extra pressure on them, they felt unable to share concerns or problems in their business with others, they were constantly confronted by challenges they were expected to sort out, and they seldom received any thanks or praise for their hard work.

Some of you may have high self-esteem around your sporting career, or your role at work, and yet low self-esteem in your social life or family environment. If we feel vulnerable, or at risk, we are more susceptible to accepting a criticism, or a put down, which in more secure circumstances we would never sanction.

The saying goes that "sticks and stones may break my bones but words will never hurt me". That may well ring true if you are someone with high all round self-esteem; for you are likely to reject the verbal arrows sent your way.

Sadly, many of us have been prone to damaging our self-esteem by sanctioning the negative opinions of parents, authorities, and experts who did not realise the harm they were doing.

Children who receive genuine praise, who are helped to develop an expectation that they will enjoy each day, and are encouraged to feel good about themselves, are likely to develop a confidence and resilience that will stand them in good stead.

You can instil the same traits in yourself with simple mental exercises performed daily and I will come back to this in a later chapter.

Finally, I offer a word of warning if you are a perfectionist. What do you do after completing a task? Do you focus on the 99.5% you did well, or on the 0.5% that was not perfect? The chances are that you beat yourself up over the latter, and forget to acknowledge yourself for the former.

Acknowledging your achievements, albeit with due modesty, is often considered inappropriate, too embarrassing, or simply not part of the family or organisational culture. I urge you to acknowledge and celebrate your success in sport, at home, and at work whenever possible and suitable – you may need to do it silently inside your own head if a more public statement or celebration is not appropriate.

Developing a healthy level of self-esteem and self-efficacy, in areas in which you wish to excel, is one of the most significant keys to fulfilling your potential.

Develop self-efficacy for others

Regrettably, most of us have been, or still are, self-destructive when giving feedback to ourselves. Earlier, I urged you to be careful about your self-talk. Giving helpful feedback to ourselves, or others, revolves around awareness of the significance of self-talk. You will often have heard people saying things like "There I go again, I always screw up when I try to…", or "Look at the mess I made of parking the car in that huge space – I've never been any good at it".

When people underperform, or do what they should not, the important thing is that they hear what is expected of them (from you or from themselves), and how good they are, with language like "we don't live like that, the next time do it this way", or "that's not like you, you usually do that really well".

If you are giving the feedback, provided the person you are speaking to sees you as an authority, or an expert, they will hopefully sanction your view and put a positive weight on their attitudinal balance scale (a concept I will expand on in the 'Effective 'mind games" chapter).

Constructive feedback

On the subject of giving feedback to someone, I would like to share with you two examples of techniques that have helped me many times.

The first example is from work inspired by Titus Alexander, the founder of the 'Self-esteem Network', a charity of which I was very happy to be a trustee.

We coined the acronym 'BE FAIR' as a guide to giving effective feedback to others when their behaviour upsets us.

B to describe the Behaviour in question
E to explain the Effect the behaviour has on you
F to convey how it makes you Feel
A to suggest an Alternative approach/behaviour for the future
I to Invite their reaction/response to your suggestion.
R to Receive their feedback in a constructive way.

Try this approach for yourself, or your own variety of it, and see how often you are able to achieve a comfortable and mutually beneficial outcome.

Non-threatening feedback

When feedback is delivered in a way that makes you feel under threat, or accused, your instinctive response is often to counterattack and the conversation then becomes adversarial and counterproductive.

A simple process for keeping the conversation positive, and fruitful, is known as 'Feel, Want, Willing'.

This is a technique that may take you a little practice to perfect, as it involves the following four-stage approach *WITHOUT YOU EVER USING THE WORD 'YOU'*:

1. Describe how a situation makes you **feel**;
2. Explain what change you **want** to see achieved as an alternative;
3. State what you are **willing** to do to achieve the change;
4. **Then stop talking** and wait for their reply.

Listening to such an approach (which has at no point sounded critical, judgemental or threatening – because the word 'you' was never used) usually leaves the recipient able to assess the proposal calmly.

Almost invariably this will promote a positive response in which the other party involved will instinctively give you their equivalent suggestions and you have the beginnings of a discussion on how to resolve the (often long-standing) situation to your mutual benefit.

I explained this concept one afternoon to a very senior director of a multinational company. He commented that there was another member of the board of directors with whom he had had a very difficult relationship for many years. It had reached the point whereby, if he knew they needed to meet or talk, he would find himself spontaneously visualising the disagreeable conversation that he saw as inevitable.

The following day, when we resumed the coaching session, he named a colleague of his and asked if I had either coached him or taken him through a workshop. When I said I had done neither he expressed astonishment.

He explained that when this colleague, who was the fellow director he had been in conflict with for so long, had telephoned him out of the blue the previous evening he had decided to try out the 'feel, want, willing' approach. For the first time ever they had had a really productive conversation as, to his surprise, his colleague had responded along such similar lines that he thought I must have taught him the same technique.

I was delighted that he had found an opportunity so quickly to try out the approach and that it had been so successful.

From that example, something you may want to be alert to from now on is catching yourself 'looking forward' to something, with a negative expectation, because in the past that experience, or your meeting with an individual, has always gone badly.

If there have been bad experiences in the past, it is all the more reason to prepare constructively for the next occasion, and to consider whether giving those involved some (constructive) feedback would be helpful.

When I first had this concept explained to me, I could think of a number of contacts from my past, some colleagues and some clients, where meetings had consistently been less productive than I would have liked and where the technique would have been well worth trying.

Now that I know these two feedback techniques, and am careful not to have negative expectations of any meetings, conversations go a lot better. I do recommend the approach to you strongly.

I am not suggesting you currently have many difficult conversations, but you never know when you may need to get your feelings across to a colleague at work, or to one of your coaches, or perhaps to an Olympic official, without their taking offence that you are standing up for yourself and your rights.

I am, however, surprised at how often, when helping people with mental preparation for a challenging situation, I need to stress the idea that it is important that they look forward, with a positive expectation, to a desirable outcome.

Stretch your goals

I will elaborate, in the 'Effective 'mind games" chapter, on the fact that your subconscious has the capacity to work very effectively in support of you achieving your goals, provided you know how to 'put your mind to it'.

For now, you need to know that one key to this is maintaining as much distance as possible between your current level of performance and the performance level you are aspiring to.

This does not work for you if, like Walter Mitty, you fantasise about achieving things that are way beyond your existing subconscious self-efficacy.

It is really important therefore, that you find a coach who is able to monitor it for you, so that you can set your sights on the upper limit of that inner self-belief and subsequently boost it, on an ongoing basis, as it is likely to increase steadily as your performance improves.

Understanding how your mind works will encourage you to stretch your goals and use 'mind games' to help you achieve them. I will be giving you some specific suggestions later in the book but one thing that is important for you to understand at this point is the concept of Gestalt.

Gestalt

You may have noticed that when you see something that looks out of order to you, whether that be a picture that is crooked on the wall, litter on the floor, or a job unfinished, you have an instinctive need to 'put things right'.

It seems we all have this built-in need to make things how we think they should look, or should be, and that need often triggers a sense of urgency to straighten out the mess. That is an illustration of Gestalt.

That is not to say that everyone will straighten pictures, pick up rubbish, or complete jobs. Only when those outcomes are important to us, or we recognise that they are our responsibility, will the need for action get through our RAS (the filter system we looked at earlier in the book). When we feel accountable to resolve the problem, we will only be content when we have restored things to how we think they should be.

This is Gestalt at work. You can use this instinct to your advantage when you need help to tackle a problem. Provided you can get others to see your point of view, that things are not 'as they should be' and need fixing for example, then they will be as energised as you are to solve the problem and get things looking right.

Children may even help with the washing up if it means that, once it is done, their parents will be available to play with them or take them somewhere they are keen to go.

This energised drive fits well with an illustration that I often use to explain the benefits of having an ideal 'stretch' goal that is set at the top limit of your self-efficacy.

Imagine one end of a rubber band being pegged at the current performance level, and the other end extended to the goal, thereby creating tension. The greater the tension you can create by increasing the gap between the two, the greater the subconscious drive, energy, and creativity to close the gap.

Clearly if you stretch the rubber band too far (metaphorically beyond your self-efficacy), it will snap. Equally, as your performance improves the gap lessens – and with it the tension (and therefore the level of drive and energy).

For me, two conclusions follow from this idea. Firstly, that if you can persuade your mind that the success you would like to have is how things ought to look, then that will trigger Gestalt to make the success happen.

Secondly, that you need to consider revising and extending your personal or team goals before you reach the current target. By so doing you will ensure that tension is maintained in the 'rubber band' to maintain your drive and energy.

The last essential thing to understand, and this is the final key to why 'mind games' will work for you, is that, fortunately for you, your mind does not distinguish between an experience that has actually happened to you and something that you very vividly imagine experiencing.

This is often the reason behind those conversations where one person says they did do something they were meant to do and another party flatly contradicts them.

I well remember being dumbfounded some years ago when I was working in an office. The wife of the man who used the desk next to me telephoned, needing to speak to him urgently, and I promised I would get him to ring her. I knew he would be returning to the office shortly and could imagine him walking through the doors and my passing on the message.

The next day he gave me an enormous rocket for failing to tell him to ring his wife. Because I had so clearly pictured myself passing the message to him, I was convinced that I had done so and we had one of those "yes I did", "no you didn't" conversations which I did not understand until I learnt about this concept.

In the chapter on 'mind games', I will suggest you use a technique that makes use of this aspect of how your mind works. By mentally rehearsing the attainment of the improvement you are seeking on a regular basis, and in an appropriate way, that successful experience will become part of your self-image, which in turn will generate that success or behaviour as being just naturally what you do.

High achievers are constantly thinking about how they want their lives to be and I have already suggested a number of reasons why this helps them to succeed.

To use more of your potential, I suggest you make use of these concepts and aspire to great heights of pleasure and success, knowing that life will confront you with the contrasting current reality and Gestalt will thereby be triggered to 'put things right'.

You will be drawn to whatever pictures you choose to dwell on in your mind and your RAS will be opened to resources that will help you achieve your goals.

So in closing this chapter, I hope you have gained enough insights on how your mind works to understand why the 'mind games' that I will describe in the final chapter will work for you if you apply them properly.

I also hope that I have highlighted sufficiently the benefits of the 'Mindset Priming' approach that I will be describing in the next chapter, and that you have already decided to find someone who can check how high you can set your goals, and whether or not you have some subconscious resistance that needs to be removed for you.

Before leaving this section on Gestalt a word of warning in case any of you have eyesight like mine.

For years, when staying in friends' homes, if I saw a crooked picture (and I often did) I would helpfully straighten it. When my wife and I first furnished a home together I was surprised that she hung all the pictures crooked and I therefore naturally straightened them.

My wife, fairly forcefully, asked me what on earth I thought I was doing. On hearing my explanation she marched off and returned with a spirit level with which she very effectively demonstrated that every picture was now tilting to the right.

Now, when visiting or staying with friends, if it looks to me as if their pictures are tilting to the left (just like ours at home) I leave well alone – with a twinge of embarrassment as I think of all the pictures I 'straightened' with such good intentions for so many years.

I do comfort myself that my actions were well intentioned, but now leave people to live their lives in their own way, in their own homes – if it looks OK to them that is all that matters!

Actions steps for you to take:

Decide to be aware of your self-talk and correct any that is counterproductive.

Be sure to give yourself and others constructive feedback.

Build your self-efficacy by acknowledging your achievements and progress.

Raise your goals to the limit of what you can 'see yourself doing' to trigger Gestalt.

Stretch your goals following a new level of success (ideally with the help of a suitably trained coach) to maintain drive and energy.

(You can find how to contact those trained in this approach via my website:
www.pathfindersabc.co.uk)

If you are interested in discovering how to help those in your organisation, hospital, school, college, or community to use these concepts to unleash their potential and tackle challenges more easily, then contact me, if in the UK, or else The Pacific Institute®,
www.thepacificinstitute.com
They have offices all over the world and would be happy to help you.

Part 3
My Kinesiology experience

"I've done a lot of work with Jeremy, and his integrated approach takes sports psychology to a new and even more powerful level. I would recommend him to any competitor, at any level, wishing to achieve their full potential.

What interests me, more than just the psychology side of what he does, is the kinesiology, which is really interesting, in that you get right to the nub of what your worries, concerns, and fears might be, as you are really tapping into your subconscious.

So at the end of the session, you know you've dealt with the problems that you need to, if you're going to perform to the best of your ability."

Goldie Sayers,
GB javelin record holder
UK javelin champion for 10 years

Developing the approach

The key points:

The coaching approach I have developed, and use with Olympic and Paralympic athletes, is a combination of Cognitive psychology and 3-in-1 Concepts kinesiology that works at the physical, emotional, and psychological levels.

'The Pinnacle of Success' model helps by illustrating the links between the four elements of the 'ABC' model and the many levels of our consciousness.

'Mindset Priming' is an entry level coaching approach that helps you set the most appropriate goal(s), gives you access to the root causes of any self-imposed limitations on your aspirations and performance, and identifies the best 'mind games' to improve your performance.

'Mind/Body Alignment' is a more profound, holistic approach that can also address your imbalances at a physical as well as an emotional or psychological level and thus, while powerful for all, is likely to be especially valuable for those competing in the Paralympics or Invictus Games.

You can work with 'mind games' on your own, but will need someone trained in some kinesiology techniques to help you with these two approaches.

I qualified to teach an advanced level of kinesiology in 1985. If you have not previously come across kinesiology it is a complementary therapy that can benefit everyone (and is quite different from kinesiology tape used in sports).

Blending Eastern and Western medical thinking, it enables the therapist to identify imbalances in their clients' energy systems and to rectify those imbalances. This simple balancing approach can have a profound and lasting impact on the physical and/or emotional wellbeing of the clients.

Roger Black tells me that he and Steve Backley were both helped in their athletic preparations by a kinesiologist.

All branches of kinesiology use a process that I shall call 'monitoring' to get feedback from the client which indicates what work needs to be done, which techniques will be the most appropriate, and when the balance has been completed.

My introduction to kinesiology

When I first saw a demonstration of kinesiology, I was at a stage of my life when I needed to understand how something worked before I believed that it would work. I well remember watching the instructor invite someone to come forward from the audience who had an emotional trauma they would like help with.

The lady who volunteered described, in a tearful and shaking voice, how some years earlier she had been walking in London, with her small child holding onto her hand, when he had stepped off the curb and been fatally run over by a bus. I was stunned to hear her, no more than 15 or 20 minutes later, describe the event again in a strong clear voice without a tear in sight. All the instructor had done was to use a simple technique that he described as 'emotional stress diffusion' that involved no more than his holding the lady's head (front and back) while she ran the traumatic scenario in her imagination again a few times.

A succession of volunteers from the audience then came forward with a variety of physical issues and I watched as they had their headaches removed, or pain reduced, by the instructor working on pressure points or acupuncture meridians and, as he explained it, 'balancing their energy meridians'.

My reaction was that I had no idea how it was possible to relieve physical and emotional pain so easily but, for once, I couldn't care how it worked, I just wanted to learn how to do it.

One thing I loved about kinesiology, from the start, was that it put the client in charge of whether it was appropriate to work with them, and if so with what focus, and in what way.

The monitoring process can be relied on to indicate what it is appropriate to do, and how to measure progress being made.

When people ask me whether I will be able to help them, or someone they know, with a particular pain or problem, I am always careful to answer "I don't know". Just because I have helped one or more people with, say, arthritic pain does not mean that the next person with that condition will have the same outcome.

The Kinesiology Federation

Twenty-five years ago I was elected the inaugural vice-chair of the Kinesiology Federation (KF) – then made up of a small group of different branches of kinesiology, whose leaders all wanted to ensure a consistency and quality of the training available to students. We were also determined to raise awareness of the wide-ranging benefits of the therapy.

When, a while later, a House of Lords committee

evaluated a range of complementary therapies, we in the KF were disappointed not to be grouped with those approved for use in the NHS (ironically the reason being in part because a kinesiology treatment will always be varied to suit each patient, rather than identical for all those with a particular condition).

We were grateful nonetheless to receive a letter from one of the peers on the committee expressing his personal regret and assuring us that he would continue to use it himself in his dental practice as he knew how well it worked.

Now the KF is a thriving organisation with many members representing a wide range of kinesiologies, professionals, and students.

Over the many years that I have sought to help people with this approach, there have been a few times when it was not appropriate to work at all and there have been many times when extraordinary results have been achieved.

Although I specialised in helping people with dyslexia, I had success working on clients with the widest possible variety of conditions and challenges, from someone with ME, to a lady desperate to have a child (following a number of miscarriages), people with career concerns, and elite competitors with sporting challenges.

My favourite process

Of particular interest to those of you who are serious competitors is one of my favourite applications of this therapy that is called 'a goal balance'.

This involves the client picking a date in the future and describing in as much detail as possible what they see as the ideal picture of how their life could be at that time.

The next stage is to use the monitoring process to

check whether the picture of the ideal future lodged in their unconscious mind would enhance their conscious picture.

This is precisely the technique I have been using with Olympic prospects and, as mentioned in the chapter on 'Raising the bar', it has come as no surprise to me that, without exception, every athlete's unconscious self-belief (in the speed that they can run, or the distance they can throw) has been greater than their conscious ambition.

Having used the monitoring process to set a stretched goal that the client is excited about at the conscious and unconscious levels, it comes as no surprise that the first measurement invariably shows 100% commitment to that goal.

What intrigues me is that with only one exception so far, the second measurement has revealed levels of resistance of up to 100% (triggered perhaps by self-doubt, fear of failure, fear of success, past memories, expectations etc.) lurking in the client's subconscious.

This resistance can always be cleared with kinesiology techniques (and other therapies and approaches may also be effective). It may take a number of sessions to clear it completely but the impact on the client is remarkable.

There is an almost visible level of excitement and determination when the monitoring process indicates to them that they are 100% committed to their goal and that there is no resistance, at any level of consciousness, to inhibit their progress.

There are too many techniques, which one can use when 'balancing' someone with kinesiology, to list in this book. The best way to give you a sense of what can be achieved is to offer some case studies.

I could describe many sessions that I have had with clients to illustrate the effectiveness and reliability of the goal balancing process, but I will limit myself at this stage to one example where the goal setting element was significant, and a second example where the goal setting aspect, and reducing the resistance, were both unusual.

Two examples of a 'goal balance'

Very early on in my kinesiology career, a lady came to see me who had discussed with her partner the prospect of their sharing a home together within the next couple of years. Both of them had been married before and had children.

The monitoring process helped her to pick a date about 18 months ahead and she began to describe what she saw as the ideal picture of their life together at that time. When I came to check what her unconscious view was of the picture she had just come up with, the monitoring indicated that something was missing. After a great deal further testing we discovered that her unconscious was seeing another child in the picture.

To my concern she became extremely agitated and was adamant that she would not be having another child. Repeated testing produced the same answer – that there would be another child in the picture by the date on which we were focusing. Each time that answer emerged her distress increased (and this was contrary to all my previous experience as the process had always previously been stress-free and fun for the client).

Suddenly she became quite calm and asked me to remind her of the dates we were talking about. When I did so, she gave a deep sigh and said, "That's quite extraordinary. At that time my sister will be on her travels going round the world and I've promised that I will look after her daughter while she is away".

The 'missing child' had been her niece all along (not a new baby of her own). The need for the child to be in the picture had been lodged in her memory, and her unconscious mind knew full well that the picture she was imagining would not be complete until she had remembered that her niece would be staying, at that time, with her and her partner.

The second example I want to share with you involves a patient whose doctor sent him to me after he had been diagnosed with cancer for the second time (I had got to know him when working with him after the earlier diagnosis).

The monitoring process indicated that a goal balance was the most appropriate procedure and a date was selected two years ahead. Asked to describe how his life would ideally be then, his answer was that everything was black.

He could see no future and clearly believed that he would be dead by then. I had worked with him for some weeks and, as he was thoroughly familiar with the approach, I light-heartedly told him that he might as well start creating a picture of his future, even if it meant making things up, as he would not be able to leave my clinic until the monitoring process confirmed that our session was completed.

With the help of the monitoring process we were able to build up a picture of his future in which he would be living abroad with his family and benefiting from a different climate. Once we had established that he was 100% committed to this picture, I began working on reducing the significant level of resistance in his subconscious.

Unusually the testing indicated that I should not tell him which of his doubts or concerns I was working on, so I simply carried out a succession of processes (that the monitoring prioritised for me) from the kinesiology options available to me.

At the end of the session he, therefore, completely unaware that I had spent a considerable time working on the origins of fears in his mind. Fears not so much that he might die, but fears linked to his concern about the distress and devastation that his death would cause his family.

He happened to leave his watch behind in the clinic that evening and he came round to my home to collect it the next morning. To my amazement and delight his opening words were "I've no idea what you did last night but the fear has all gone".

I can confirm that I heard recently, many years later, that he and his family were thriving in the country that he had chosen in that goal balancing session.

Working with kinesiology

So, what is a session like? It is reassuring that as a coach, or therapist, when working with kinesiology you can use the monitoring process to identify and prioritise each step in the session.

To help you get a sense of what the process feels like I often compare it to when you go to a restaurant and are offered a menu that is many pages long and has several options on each page. You decide how many courses you want to eat, which pages on the menu are relevant to choose from, and which dishes from each page will suit you on that particular occasion.

Similarly, when visiting a kinesiologist, the monitoring process, using an approach sometimes called 'asking the body questions', makes it possible for you to identify what support you need, from a series of menus, that offer many wide-ranging procedures that between them will correct the temporary, and potentially inhibiting, imbalances in your system.

After I began to blend my kinesiology work with the psychological concepts that I taught, I realised that all those kinesiologists that use the 'asking the body questions' approach can readily adapt their processes to work with all levels of 'Escalating Coaching' and 'Mindset Priming'.

As they already use the 'menu' approach, that lets the client select what they need on each visit, they could easily add a 'menu' of psychological concepts to those they were already working with.

I wanted people to be able to picture the different, and integrated, levels at which the process works. I also wanted a model that could be used, at the end of a balance, to check that there is no residual stress, or trauma, that needs to be cleared from any facet or level.

I therefore adapted the 'ABC of Success' model into what I call 'The Pinnacle of Success' to help my students and clients understand how all four 'ABC' elements interact with their many levels of consciousness.

The 'Pinnacle of Success' model

If you bring the four elements of the 'ABC of Success' model together like this, you have an equilateral triangle with 'Behaviour' in the centre, flanked by 'Conditioning' and 'Aspirations', with 'Description of yourself' underneath.

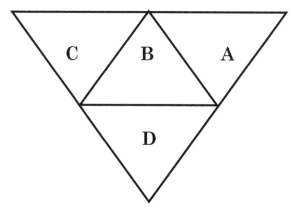

If you then imagine that there are hinges all around the 'Behaviour' triangle, by folding up the other three elements, you end up with a three-dimensional shape in which each side is connected to all of the other three:

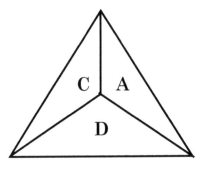

There is an interaction that takes place within us all not only between each of the four faces of the Pinnacle but also between each level of consciousness.

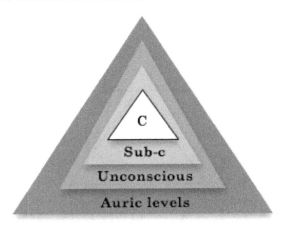

This diagram illustrates how each of the four faces has concentric triangles with the conscious level of thought in the centre, progressing through the subconscious level to the unconscious level, and out to the many auric levels beyond.

When clearing the trauma from past memories, the model makes it easy for the client to understand what level the trauma has impacted.

In every session the monitoring process lets each client recognise how the selected techniques are tailored to their precise needs, and the 'Pinnacle of Success' model helps them to understand that any imbalances in their mind/body neurology have been suitably addressed.

For the aspiring super stars wanting to know about applications of the process with competitors in a range of sports, I will describe (with the kind approval of those involved) some case studies in the later chapter on 'Escalating Coaching'.

I will describe how the process helped the British javelin champion, Goldie Sayers, before she competed in the World Championships in 2015, some athletes preparing for the 2016 Olympics, and also how the process helped an outstanding amateur golfer to turn pro.

Actions steps for you to take:

If you are a UK sports competitor, you can contact me via my website to find a suitable coach near you who could give you a 'Goal balance' or a 'Mindset Priming' session.

If you would like to study kinesiology in the UK, contact me via my website to find a conveniently located and suitable instructor.

If you are a kinesiologist and interested in adding the psychological 'menu' to your current offering, contact me via my website for details of future workshops.

If you are a personal trainer, a sports psychologist, a sports coach or a life coach, and are interested to learn about 'Mindset Priming' and/or 'Escalating Coaching' contact me via my Pathfinders website for details of suitable workshops.

Relevance to Paralympians, Invictus Games competitors, and Help for Heroes patients

The key points:

A kinesiology balance will improve the integration of the client's mind/body neurology at each session.

A single balance has been known to have an impact on the mobility of severely injured patients.

Dr Charles Krebs, having been a quadriplegic after suffering from type two (cerebro-spinal) bends, learnt to walk again with the help of his neurological knowledge, determination, physical training, visualisation, and kinesiology sessions.

'Escalating Coaching' combines the kinesiological and psychological approaches that could make a difference to every client (and perhaps especially to those listed above) and helps clients adjust their visualisation to have the most impact.

Before introducing you to 'Escalating Coaching' and 'Mindset Priming', I want to explain why my experience with kinesiology leads me to think that Paralympians, those competing in the Invictus Games, and Help for Heroes patients might well benefit hugely from this approach.

While I was being trained in America to teach 3-in-1 Concepts, two of us were asked if we would demonstrate it to a former Hollywood youth star who had been devastatingly injured in a car crash. He could only walk rather grotesquely by rotating his body to get one leg in front of the other in turn.

At the end of the session he expressed himself fascinated by the process, and very grateful, but commented, rather apologetically, that he could not detect any improvement or change in his condition.

The next day he rang our instructor to thank him for sending us along and asked him to pass on the information that, following our visit, he had gone, as usual, to a friend's house to take advantage of the opportunity to swim privately in the afternoon (thinking that his appearance might cause distress to people at a public swimming pool). He said that for the past two years, since recovering from his accident, his feet had hit each other when he swam – and they did not do so any more.

I cannot, of course, be sure that it was the kinesiology session that made the difference, but I have always believed that that was the case and that firm belief was reinforced when I heard and read the story of Dr Charles Krebs.

He tells his story in the book *A Revolutionary Way of Thinking* which describes how he progressed from a near fatal diving accident to a new science of healing (based on kinesiology). The short version is that he became a quadriplegic after suffering cerebro-spinal bends (which I think of as second degree bends – far more serious than the more common first degree variety).

After an extraordinary and completely experimental treatment in a decompression chamber (which he was in for a record ten days), followed by extensive use of his knowledge of anatomy and neurology to help him to use creative visualisation, he managed to regain some movement in his limbs.

After six months of exhausting exercise activity, to regain strength in his legs, this former quadriplegic was just able to walk out of the hospital on two sticks. He walked so poorly, and fell over in the street so often, that people sometimes presumed he was drunk. Neurological tests showed that in addition to spinal damage he had also suffered damage to his frontal lobes.

Determined to overcome his disabilities, he worked with self-hypnosis, meditation, and acupuncture before a friend then introduced him to Dr Bruce Dewe, who with two other kinesiologists, worked on him for an hour and a half.

To quote from *A Revolutionary Way of Thinking*: "At the conclusion of the treatment Dewe told me to get up off the table and walk. When I first stood up I could hardly balance. I certainly couldn't walk. So much had occurred in my neurology that I couldn't walk for about 15 minutes. Then suddenly I was walking in a totally new way. Instead of arching my hips and dragging my feet, I was walking with my feet aligned under my hips. It was a massive functional change. Something profound had happened. I was walking in a much more efficient way than I had been able to in the more than two years that had passed since the accident. Dewe was working from a model that said something could change and it had. My model said that what had happened was impossible. But it had happened."

When he visited the UK recently I made a point of attending one of his lectures and was astonished by the comparative ease with which he walked to the platform and delivered his presentation. Talking with him afterwards I heard more about his most remarkable recovery and about his ongoing interest in kinesiology (he developed a very sophisticated method of helping people with learning difficulties which is known as LEAP).

What struck me, when I first read his story, was that Charles had started his progress with a belief that he would overcome his quadriplegia and a determination to do so. Secondly (thanks to having a very detailed knowledge of anatomy and neurology) he had spent hours visualising the energy flowing down his limbs until they became active. Finally it was clear that that the kinesiology session had quite dramatically stimulated the reintegration of the connection between his mind and body.

In the chapter of this book entitled 'Mental simulation', I will go into considerable detail about the use of visualisation – both how to use it and also, importantly, why it works. Properly used it is such a powerful process that I have made that chapter of the book freely available, through the website, so that all athletes/competitors/people seeking to make changes in their circumstances can access it easily and start to use it for themselves.

Reading Charles's book I realised how well my integrated approach would be likely to support others embarking on this kind of recovery – it starts with your inner belief in what you could do, deals with subconscious doubts and concerns, rebalances your mind/body interaction and teaches you how to visualise your way to the achievement of your goal.

I am not for a moment suggesting that it is a cure-all approach for all those recovering from trauma but I would love the opportunity for its benefits to be researched by those working in that field.

Actions steps for you to take:

If you are a Paralympian, or Invictus Games competitor, seek help from appropriately trained coaches or kinesiologists.

If you are coaching these competitors, discover more about the potential benefits of kinesiology and 'Escalating Coaching'.

If you work with, or have connections with, Help for Heroes, then do encourage them to investigate what kinesiology, or appropriate coaching, might do for their patients.

'Escalating Coaching' and 'Mindset Priming'

The key points:

The first step of 'Mindset Priming' will enable your coach to prioritise those psychological concepts that you will find helpful in order to fulfil your potential.

The second step gives your coach the basic tools with which to help you stretch your aspirations.

The third step would equip your coach to identify and reduce subconscious fears, concerns, and doubts that may be lurking at the back of your mind and inhibiting your self-belief and success.

'Mindset Priming' also equips your coach to identify the most appropriate 'mind games' that will help you to improve your performance and get 'in the zone' when competing.

Those trained to the more advanced levels of 'Escalating Coaching' can work even more profoundly to improve your mind/body alignment with your goals.

I have described how in kinesiology the monitoring process works in a similar way to someone choosing nourishing food from the pages of a restaurant menu.

It is sometimes referred to as 'asking the body questions' and it is almost like a waiter in the restaurant asking the customer, "What would suit you today?" and the customer responding, "Given my needs, I would just like these two starters please" or "The soup followed by the fish and then the fruit salad please" – whatever they think would nourish them on the day.

I have also mentioned how I came to trust the process, even though I did not have a complete idea of how it worked, and even though it appeared at times to defy what the medical world believes is possible.

A few years ago, I decided to explore the possibility of incorporating psychological concepts into my kinesiology approach. I contacted people who had attended workshops I had facilitated on practical applications of cognitive psychology.

The four 'insights'

I grouped the psychological concepts into what I called four insights:

- When do we limit our aspirations?
- What four things hold us back from achieving our goals?
- Why are improvements so often temporary?
- What do instinctively successful people do to maintain progress?

I asked for feedback on which of the concepts had been of the most value to the many former participants to whom I emailed the list.

Most of those I had emailed took the trouble to reply and once I had pulled together a list of what seemed, from their responses, to be the most significant concepts, I mentally added this to my 'Pinnacle of Success' process.

I have been delighted with the number of times, when working with my individual clients, that the monitoring process has indicated that they need to understand one of the psychological concepts, or indeed a blend of them, in order to bring about the changes they are seeking.

'Mindset Priming' works for golfers

I now call the new approach 'Mindset Priming' and am delighted that it has appealed so strongly to those in the field of international sports (and athletics in particular).

It enables you to discover your inner belief about your potential, adjust your goals accordingly, and eliminate doubts and fears lurking in your subconscious.

To give you an example of how rapidly a competitor's performance can improve when their self-belief has increased, I well remember working with Darren Lovegrove, an outstanding young amateur golfer, who wanted to turn pro but whose handicap had been stuck at 1.8 for a while.

Before relating the improvements he achieved in his game and in his handicap, it is worth specifically describing key elements of our first two sessions, as they again illustrate the value and accuracy of the monitoring process.

We initially worked on making him consciously aware of his subconscious beliefs about his accuracy and consistency with each of his clubs and this changed his expectations of success – especially on his short game.

In our first session, his subconscious identified that the priority to work on was his putter. His coach had had him practising six foot putts, but his subconscious belief was that he was capable of a high success rate with eight foot putts, and therefore that was the preferred distance for him to practise. His coach was happy for him to make that change and we waited to see what the monitoring identified as the focus for the second session.

Again the focus was on a club but this time it was his pitching wedge (for any non-golfers reading this, that would be the club most often used to get the ball onto the green before putting it in the hole). As it had been with his putter, his inner belief in his potential accuracy with his wedge was far greater than the conscious idea he had 'in his head'.

What was remarkable, given the outcome of the first session, was that the monitoring indicated that he could expect a high percentage of shots with his pitching wedge to land within eight feet of the hole – the exact range he had identified earlier from which he had a strong prospect of needing just one putt.

Combining the feedback from the monitoring on the two sessions he could calculate that, if playing to his current skill level, once his pitching wedge was in his hand he could expect to complete the hole in just two shots something like 60% of the time.

Having established his new aspirations for his game we monitored, and reduced, the subconscious resistance to the new success levels and thereby boosted his expectations and his confidence.

In subsequent sessions, we worked on his confidence and expectations with the other clubs in his bag. We also worked on his expectations of his total scores on courses where he regularly competed and on his thoughts about which holes to hope to birdie. Once particular holes were suggested to him by his own subconscious, as being holes that he was good enough to birdie (given reasonable weather conditions), he was able to reassess his strategy for playing those holes and courses.

We were both delighted that within just two weeks of my starting to work with him his handicap had reduced from 1.8 to 0.6 and soon after that it had dropped far enough for him to be able to turn pro – happily for me he was taken on as a coach at my local golf club and he has helped me to improve my own game for many years.

'Mindset Priming' works for athletes

Having been told after the 2012 London Olympics that I should be training Great Britain's athletics coaches (and working with the athletes myself), I set about seeking to make contact with influential people at that level.

I was eventually introduced to Steve Backley (himself a legendary Olympic medallist and javelin record holder) who introduced me to Goldie Sayers who for many years has been our top women's javelin thrower, having first competed in the Olympic Games in 2004, and whose British record stands at over 66 metres.

Having missed a medal in Beijing in 2008 by 38 centimetres, she then in 2012, having just improved on her British record, was unable to do herself justice in the London Olympics after a horrific injury to her throwing arm.

In spite of a subsequent knee injury, she was determined to compete at the top level again in the World Championships in Beijing in 2015 and in the Olympics in Rio in 2016.

When I started working with her in June 2015 she had only recently resumed training and she still needed to throw the qualifying distance if she was going to be able to represent Great Britain in the World Championships which were due to be held that August.

She came to see me with just over a month to go before the last qualifying competition. She was then throwing just 45 metres, from a walk rather than a run, and consciously expecting, when fitter, to throw 60 or 61 metres.

At the start of our session, the monitoring process revealed that her unconscious self-belief was that she could throw 62 metres but also registered a high level of subconscious resistance to that belief.

We worked (using kinesiological techniques, selected psychological concepts, and some energy work) until we had reduced her resistance level to zero and then, on a whim, decided to check the distance that she now believed she could throw at the unconscious level. We were both surprised and delighted that the picture of how far she could throw (if fully fit by then) had increased from 62 metres to 65 metres as a result of removing the resistance that had been lurking at the back of her mind.

She is a very determined and courageous lady and by our next session late in July, with the trials just a couple of days ahead, she was able to throw off a full run (although not yet fully fit).

At the start of the session her conscious goal for the World Championships was to finish in the top three and at the subconscious level the monitoring process showed her that she could see herself achieving a new personal best throw in excess of 66 metres.

At the end of the session, having removed all subconscious resistance – again with several psychological concepts as well as kinesiological techniques – she saw a realistic goal being to throw more than 64 metres at the qualifying event in two days' time and to throw a personal best of 67 metres in the World Championships in August.

She duly qualified for the World Championships, and represented Great Britain in Beijing, but cruelly her knee injury returned and she was unable to do herself justice.

Since the first edition of this book appeared, in spite of working on her physical recovery with a coach in the USA, and having further sessions of 'Escalating Coaching' with me on her return to the UK, her injuries prevented her being ready for the Olympics in Rio and she has now retired from competition.

She was kind enough to make this comment on the work we did together:

> *The subconscious is an often untapped resource in the world of sports psychology. Your integrated approach takes sports psychology to a new and even more powerful level. I would recommend you to any competitor, at any level, wishing to achieve their full potential. Thanks again for your tremendous support.*

Having worked with Goldie it seemed clear to me that I could give valuable help to anyone competing in a single athletic event.

Thinking back to Darren, and the work we did on all the different shots that were involved in his competitions, it struck me that it would also be really interesting to work with, for example, a modern pentathlete, or heptathlete, where raising their inner self-belief for each event in their competition would be significant.

I believe that increasing such an athlete's confident expectations of success, across the full range of their events, would have a dramatic impact on their overall score and I am hoping to have the opportunity to prove the benefits of the approach with some of them before long.

What I learnt from working with athletes

Before she left to recuperate and train in America, Goldie introduced me to Jonas Dodoo, an athletics coach with a strong squad of sprinters who train at Lee Valley, and it was there that I discovered how little psychological support was available to our bright young prospects.

Working with them was a serious eye-opener for me because, although many of them were genuine prospects for the Indoor Championships in March 2016, the Olympics later that year, and the World Championships in London in 2017, only one of them had received any psychological support or training from the British Athletics movement.

Without describing our sessions in detail, here are some of their comments on the work we did together:

I worked with Jordan Kirby when he was a 22-year-old 200 metres runner with a personal best time of 20.77 seconds and he wanted to achieve a time that put him on the world stage. His comments were:

> *I liked the 'Mindset Priming' sessions and now I am more open to the idea of running faster than I think I can! I also recognise that I don't need to be the favourite in order to win. I am keen to have a later coaching session to see if I could stretch my goals and also to attend a workshop on mental preparation for success – meanwhile I will stop trying to coerce myself into being successful.*

Sean Safo-Antwi is one of Britain's top sprinters with a personal best 100 metres time of 10.14 seconds, when we first worked together. He had high hopes of 60 metres success in the Indoor Championships in 2016, was aiming to run under 10 seconds for the 100 metres before the end of year, and to be in the Olympic relay team. His comments on our sessions were:

> *What you told me was very important. I now understand the significance of visualising success and will start doing mental preparation. 'Mindset Priming' was very relevant to me in helping me achieve my goals and objectives and I am keen to have a follow-up session soon.*

When I first worked with Reece Prescod, he was a 19-year-old 200 metres runner with a personal best time of 20.7 seconds. He was hoping to run under 20 seconds and qualify for the Olympics in 2016. After our sessions he said:

> *'Mindset Priming' was hugely relevant to me in achieving my goals. I have now set myself more ambitious targets and I'm very keen to have a later session to see if I can stretch my goals further. The sessions have unblocked my inner self-belief, removed negative energy, and given me a clear mindset.*

The initial sessions I had with each of them were too short to completely remove the resistance to their potential achievements. Nevertheless, in every case, I was, with the help of the monitoring process, at least able to put them in touch with their inner self-belief and help them to raise their aspirations and expectations.

Time and again the monitoring indicated that what they needed was one, or often several, of the concepts on the psychological 'menu' explained and made relevant to them. Their evaluations of the follow-up work I did later all confirmed that they wanted more help with their mental preparation, and more coaching sessions as the year progressed, to keep them in touch with their inner self-belief in what they can realistically aspire to and prepare for.

Some of them are students, some of them are working, but they are all dedicated to their training – and that does not leave a great deal of time for additional sessions such as 'Mindset Priming'.

My experience with them has convinced me that there is enormous value in helping to raise a competitor's self-belief, and aspirations, even without removing all their subconscious doubts. They mostly also need to be taught them how to do themselves justice and be 'in the zone' at the highest levels of competition.

Reflecting on their needs, and time constraints, I realised that I needed to make it easy for coaches to gain the skills and understanding necessary to help people with these initial steps rather than with the more advanced levels of skill taught in 'Escalating Coaching'.

'Mindset Priming'

I therefore designed the step by step process that I now call 'Mindset Priming'. It can be easily taught and coaches (who need have no previous experience of kinesiology or psychology) can choose one or more steps along the training path, depending on what they want to be able to do for their protégés.

If you are a life coach, a sports coach, or a sports psychologist, I am excited that 'Mindset Priming' will add an invaluable dimension, in a number of areas, to the contribution that you are already making.

It will equip you to help clients raise their expectations of success, by putting them in touch with their unconscious self-efficacy, and measure their commitment to that higher aspiration. It will also enable you to reduce, if not necessarily remove, the subconscious resistance to their success, and it will also equip you to ensure your clients understand how to adopt the necessary mindset for the achievements they are seeking.

Finally, and importantly, you will be able to fine-tune a competitor's visualisation process, and thereby give them the best chance of adjusting their self-image and preparing for competition at the highest level.

Details of the different training steps available are given at the end of this book.

I'm not for a moment suggesting that 'Mindset Priming' on its own will be sufficient for all competitors (clearly many, if not all, would benefit from having all their subconscious sabotage demonstrably removed) but it is a powerful tool in its own right.

The more I talk to people about the unique benefits of my approach, the more I recognise that it will benefit many individuals, in their everyday lives, as well as competitors across a really wide range of sports.

For clarity, to illustrate the difference between the levels of training available, let me put them in the context of the 'ABC of Success' model that I introduced at the start of this book.

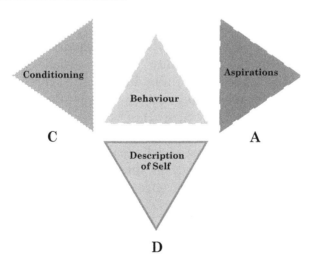

'Escalating Coaching' enables you, as a mentor, to address A, C, and D in full.

'Mindset Priming' equips you to address A and D, and also to measure how much 'C' might be inhibiting your client. It will also equip you with basic techniques that may reduce that level of resistance.

To bring this approach to the widest possible range of mentors and trainers I have created a series of workshops under the banner of 'Escalating Coaching'.

I am working to convince suitably trained kinesiologists to add the psychology element to their existing training, and thereby qualify to work with 'Escalating Coaching'.

I am doing all I can to raise awareness of both approaches, and their impact, among coaches in every imaginable sector.

Away from the world of competitive sports I have used this integrated approach when working with people in a widely differing range of circumstances.

I have helped people in senior business and government roles. I have helped teenagers heading for university. I have helped parents adjusting to their children leaving home. I have helped people being assisted by a homeless charity.

What a difference it will make when I have a host of qualified mentors ready to help people in their communities (whether individual competitors, teams, injured servicemen, students, job seekers, those in work, or re-offenders in prison, or…).

I am also looking forward to the day when I have one or more apprentices who can help me with the training workshops and, in due course, carry on my work after I choose to retire from teaching.

Actions steps for you to take:

Experience the process to see for yourself whether your current goals are set at the limit of your inner self-belief.

As a coach, decide which level of training appeals to you and apply accordingly.

As a kinesiologist, sign up for the workshop on psychological concepts/mind games and be ready to increase your client base and help our sports stars.

As a competitor, sign up for the workshop on adjusting your inner self-image and getting 'in the zone' to compete at your best.

(You can find how to contact those trained in this approach, or find out how to get trained yourself, via my website:
www.pathfindersabc.co.uk)

Part 4
Effective 'mind games'

"Nothing is impossible. With so many people saying it couldn't be done, all it takes is an imagination."

Michael Phelps,
Winner of 23 Olympic swimming gold medals

(Michael Phelps, the greatest Olympian in the history of the Games, visualises the ideal swim before he goes to sleep each night, a rigorous mental exercise in which he imagines gliding and undulating through the water in real time, stroke by stroke, divining the intimate rhythms of the perfect race.)

Putting your mind to it

The key points:

Using 'mind games' effectively is essential to ongoing/continuous improvement.

Once you know how to 'put your mind to it' you can draw on the creative power of your subconscious to accelerate your progress towards your objectives – whether they involve an improvement in your physical or emotional wellbeing, or the attainment of a specific objective or sporting triumph.

Keeping your goals stretched to the limit of your inner self-efficacy boosts your chances of success by increasing your subconscious drive and creativity.

The more you mentally rehearse the sense of the achievement of your objectives (in an effective way) the quicker your subconscious picture of yourself will adjust itself to the new you – provided your self-talk is aligned with the changes you are working on.

A natural way to change

You will probably have been told many times that you can resolve a problem, or achieve something 'if you put your mind to it'. Those telling you so were probably unaware of just how true that is.

This section of the book is really important for competitors, and other individuals, who are looking to improve their performance and/or stop restricting their success.

As some of you reading this may not yet have chosen to read the book in full, for clarity, I will briefly review some of the concepts that were covered earlier.

This part is entitled 'Effective 'mind games" because thankfully, by using visualisation, you can trick your mind into helping you to bring about the changes and improvements in performance that you want.

I questioned the value of using visualisation and affirmations for ages, until someone explained to me *why* they would work.

If this chapter alone does not give you confidence that these 'mind games' will work for you then I urge you to read the earlier chapters of this book (which I hope will provide any additional evidence you may need) or do more research into the subject.

In the coming pages I will be describing how you can 'put your mind to it' – a way to stimulate your subconscious creativity to help you bring about improvements with a process that is natural for us all and that you will find comfortable to use.

Remember that research suggests that about 15% of us are instinctively successful while the other 85% only succeed some of the time. Interestingly, the successful 15% are usually unaware that it is the way they use their mind that enables them to achieve their level of success.

Put another way, 85% of us do not know what to

do if we want to be more successful; the remaining 15% of us succeed without knowing what we're doing.

When I have been working with leadership teams in the boardrooms of large companies over the last 30 years, I have been aware that probably at least half of those present could count themselves among the 15%. Nonetheless, the most common feedback I have had, at the end of a workshop at that level, would be "Why did no-one teach me this when I was at school or at business school?".

It seems that everyone appreciates understanding the instinctive processes used by consistently successful people to make changes in their circumstances.

If you are already an elite athlete, or sports star, you may well have been encouraged to use the 'mind games' that I'm going to describe. I hope that by giving you some more background on what makes these 'mind games' effective I will encourage you to commit more time and effort to ensuring that they work for you.

The benefits of using visualisation

As Goldie Sayers puts it, "Daily visualisation should, and can be, like another training session if implemented correctly".

Many athletes have used the technique of 'mental imagery', or visualisation, to up their game and perform at their peak. *Psychology Today* reported that research on the brain patterns of weightlifters found that the patterns activated, when they lifted heavy weights, were activated similarly when they simply imagined lifting, and that some studies have even suggested that mental practice can be almost as effective as physical training.

One study, published in the *Journal of Sport & Exercise Psychology* as long ago as 1996, found that imagining weightlifting caused actual changes in muscle activity.

Visualisation has been a popular form of mental simulation since the Russian sports stars began using it in the 1970s. Now most competitors employ this technique.

Tiger Woods began using it in his pre-teen years. World champion golfer Jack Nicklaus has said "I never hit a shot, not even in practice, without having a very sharp in-focus picture of it in my head". The great former heavyweight champion, Muhammad Ali, used a blend of mental practices to improve his performance in the ring, including affirmations, visualisation, mental rehearsal, and constructive self-talk, epitomised by his famous statement, "I am the greatest".

Athletes experienced in this technique use vivid, highly detailed internal images and mental simulations of their entire performance, engaging all their senses and, where possible, combining their knowledge of the sports venue with their rehearsal.

Long before I met Steve Backley, I had read an article about him in a magazine that gave a perfect description of the results that an athlete can achieve through using the visualisation process.

He was being interviewed by a journalist, who wanted to know how it was that Steve had so often broken a record with his first throw in a competition (thereby instantly demoralising the opposition) rather than building up to a peak performance, after three or four attempts, as most competitors in field events do.

If I remember rightly, the occasion that the interviewer was most interested in was the time when Steve had broken the European record at Helsinki with his first throw. On checking the list of Steve's earlier competitions, the journalist was convinced that he had never been to Helsinki before.

Steve answered all the reporter's questions by explaining that when he discovered that he was due to compete at Helsinki, which he had neither visited nor competed at before, he had made a point of travelling there some months before the event.

He had gone to the stadium, specifically to the changing rooms, and then walked from there to the track and found the javelin throwing area. He had then taken stock of where the shot-put might be taking place, where the 110 metres hurdles might be running, where the high jump was and so on, so that on returning home he could rehearse going to the stadium, getting changed, going to the javelin area, taking his tracksuit off (with all the hubbub of other events going on around him), and breaking the record with his first throw.

By the time he arrived at Helsinki for the competition he had broken the record hundreds of times in his imagination. The experiential imagery that he had managed to use in his visualisation had been honed by the research he had done to make sure that he was picturing precisely what he would see in the competition itself.

This is a wonderful description of how visualisation can best be used to put an athlete or a competitor 'in the zone'.

It may not be possible for you to travel to every destination around the world where you will be competing, but in this technological age you may well be able to find images of the venues you hope to visit, and use those to help you with the 'mind games' that I am encouraging you to play.

Why you need to focus on what you want

It may sound obvious to say that, when embarking on making improvements or changes, it is important to start by being very clear in your mind what it is you want to achieve.

What I mean by that is that you are clear in great detail, in any aspect where change is desirable, about the results you are looking for, and the steps you will need to take, in order to achieve them.

Research tells us that we are by nature goal seekers. When we describe something we want, we get a picture of it in our mind and are drawn towards it. In fact we are drawn to whatever we're picturing, whether the picture appeals to us or not.

If you are driving a car along the road, and you see some debris in front of you, then if you keep looking at the debris the chances are that you will steer straight towards it. At some point you will realise you're about to hit it, wrench the wheel over, and drive around it.

A more comfortable journey would result from recognising there was something blocking your path ahead, immediately looking for a way past or round it, and steering in that new direction.

This principle applies to all of your goal setting. If, having decided on your destination, you can see something ahead that might get in the way of your success, I'm sure that most of you start thinking of your way around the problem, rather than focusing on the problem itself.

This leads me to hope that you are not someone who worries.

For some people, worrying seems to be a habit (and a thoroughly undesirable one). Listening to some of them I can almost imagine them worrying over the fact that they can't think of anything to worry about.

Are you someone who, when weighing up choices in front of you, focuses on and worries about some possible negative consequences of your decisions? If so, you are unlikely to be aware that you are actually increasing the chances of that unwanted outcome occurring.

Remember that we are drawn towards what we are picturing and therefore, to the extent that you keep thinking about what you don't want to happen, your subconscious will instinctively draw you towards it, like the driver heading towards the debris.

I'm not encouraging you to be like 'Little Johnny head in air' – oblivious to potential danger around you – indeed I would always encourage you to consider possible impediments to your success. I just want you to focus on the solution, not on the problem, and 'put your mind' to achieving it.

Using 'mind games' will put you in control of the improvements you want to achieve.

The coaching approach that I described earlier in the book will boost your inner belief, and confidence, by showing you what you truly believe you are capable of (at a subconscious level) and then checking for, and reducing, any doubts or concerns lurking at the back of your mind.

Once you've been helped by your coach to stretch your ambitions to the limit of your inner self-belief, or even simply set yourself some goals, there is a great deal you can do on your own to increase the likelihood that you will achieve them.

What you need to do next for yourself is to adjust your self-image to be in line with your aspiration and to prepare yourself to be 'in the zone' when competing or performing.

Before giving you the necessary techniques with which to do this, I want, in the next chapter, to explain how you can increase your commitment to the achievement of your goals.

Actions steps for you to take:

Be sure that you have a clear picture of your goals and what success will mean for you.

Get a coach to check whether you can stretch any of them.

Make sure you can 'see yourself' achieving them.

Talk to others about the benefits of using visualisation.

Satisfy yourself that using visualisation will accelerate your progress and underpin your success.

Remember to control your 'self-talk'.

If you are interested in discovering how to help those in your organisation, hospital, school, college, or community to use these concepts to unleash their potential and tackle challenges more easily, then contact me, if in the UK, or else The Pacific Institute®, www.thepacificinstitute.com.
They have offices all over the world and would be happy to help you.

Generating commitment

The key points:

Professor Bandura's research suggests that commitment has two elements: self-motivation and self-efficacy.

Focusing on the changes you want to make, in the most effective way, will boost your drive, energy, and creativity (the components of self-motivation) to find resources and solutions that will help you achieve your goals.

It is essential to raise the level of your self-belief, self-esteem, and confidence (the components of your self-efficacy) to underpin the new performance level you are striving for.

'Escalating Coaching' and 'Mindset Priming' boost your self-efficacy by highlighting your inner self-belief and removing doubts and fears from your subconscious.

Self-motivation

In the earlier part of this book I highlighted that if you want to generate commitment, you need to work on the two elements that Professor Bandura, of Stanford University, considers sit side by side – self-motivation and self-efficacy.

I want to look initially at how you can develop the three factors that combine to produce self-motivation – drive, energy and creativity. How can you generate the inner drive required for your own self-motivation?

Drive

I have heard all sorts of reasons given by Olympic competitors for wanting a gold medal. My mentoring/coaching process has enabled me to encourage them that the more challenging the goal they set the greater their drive will be.

When you choose your own goal, you automatically have the answer to the WIIFM (what's in it for me) question. The greater you perceive the benefit will be *to you,* from achieving the goal, the greater your inner drive will be.

One of the basic things that many organisational leaders get wrong is to set goals, and action plans, for other people. It is much more effective to tell a team what needs to be achieved and then let them choose the steps they will take to make that happen.

Apart from looking at *how* you plan to achieve your goal another relevant question is *why* achieving it is important to you.

If your goal is to win a gold medal, or a national event, it will probably be easy for you to identify why you want to do that.

If you are an athlete, success might mean you will gain access to sponsorship in the year ahead.

If you are part of a team, there may be all sorts of different reasons why you and your teammates would like to succeed.

One person might want their parents to be proud of them, another might want to impress their partner, another might want to see their name or photo in the paper, another might want to do better than an older sibling.

Whatever the reason, each person is striving for success, and a good coach creates an environment in which everyone in the team feels that their personal needs will be fulfilled by the attainment of the team goal.

While imposed goals seldom answer the WIIFM question, and are unlikely to generate the necessary drive, common goals within a team will often generate even more commitment, especially when freely chosen.

An interesting business example of this involved a leader seeking to motivate a team of contracting businesses who had not previously cooperated with each other. Their task was to complete, on time, two very complex and expensive phases of Ekofisk II, a North Sea oil-rig installation, for what was then Phillips Petroleum in Norway.

He told me that he had paid a substantial cash bonus after each phase. For the first phase, the cash was shared between the consortium of contractors and for the second phase, the bonus was offered to the charities of each contractor's choosing.

Feedback after the successful completion of both phases revealed that the team had been far more motivated to achieve the bonus for the charities than for themselves. Each individual had been motivated to do all they could to ensure their organisation's chosen charity received the optimum bonus (and this had given them a better feeling than merely receiving the money themselves).

In a whole range of international sports, you will often have seen extraordinary degrees of drive and determination demonstrated by individual members of a team, where they were competing not just for the glory of winning, but for their team or their nation.

Energy

What can you do to generate the maximum level of energy – the second factor in self-motivation?

At a purely physical level, it is a truism that provided you are eating healthily, and getting adequate sleep, then your energy level will be sufficient for your goals.

What is interesting and helpful to know is that drive and energy are generated, at a subconscious level, whenever your current situation falls short of how you would like things to be.

In the section of the book where I touched on Gestalt, I explained how we instinctively 'straighten up the mess' when things don't look right.

In the chapter coming up, on mental simulation, I will be explaining why deliberately imprinting a picture of success in your subconscious generates drive and energy to bring about your success, but before getting into that detail I want to look at the third factor of self-motivation – creativity – and how that can be generated.

Creativity

Earlier in the book, I introduced the Reticular Activating System as a filter mechanism for identifying elements in your environment which would help you achieve your goals. To the extent that you can get a clear picture in your mind of the outcome you are seeking to achieve, not only do you programme the filter to make you aware of solutions that are already available (if as yet unseen), you also activate your natural creative process.

The creative process has four phases. The first is to focus on the outcome you are looking for (perhaps without knowing how to achieve it) or to identify a problem.

In the second phase, called incubation, your brain scans your memory banks, and the environment, for past experiences, knowledge, or any available information that would be helpful in finding a solution.

The third phase, or illumination (you see the light), comes very often when you are deeply relaxed, maybe in the bath – like the original 'Eureka' moment – or even asleep.

I strongly recommend you keep a pad and paper, or your mobile/recording device, by your bed to capture the entirety, and perhaps the complexity, of the solution that is likely to present itself.

An astonishing example of how the entirety of your bright idea can surface from your creative subconscious happened to me some years ago.

I had for days been attempting to write a comedy sketch for a review I was appearing in. My idea was that there would be two conversations (simultaneously happening on stage between separate couples) that needed to blend together to make a third (hopefully very entertaining) conversation. I had crumpled up pages and pages of paper, attempting to create such a script, and then one night, I woke at about 3 a.m. and wrote eight sides of A4 paper, not one word of which needed changing before the sketch was performed – thankfully my subconscious creative process had been working overtime.

The fourth and final phase of the creative process is usually ignored, as people rush in to the boss, or their spouse, with their 'bright idea' only to have it shot down for lack of thought on how best it could be presented.

If there are other people involved in your project, then once the solution has presented itself to you, I suggest you apply the first three phases again in search of a good way to present your 'bright idea' to them. That will give you a chance to come up with a creative means of presenting your original solution in a way that will be understood, and is more likely to be accepted, by the others involved.

Let's move on to look at what you have already done to develop your self-efficacy, and how you can continue to do so.

Self-efficacy

Professor Bandura suggests that the other element of commitment is self-efficacy – the belief of an individual, or team, in their ability to achieve a specific goal – and that self-efficacy is a combination of belief, self-esteem, and confidence.

For those of you already competing at an elite level I am guessing that many of you first aspired to this level of performance when you were a youngster.

I would also suspect that at that young age, while you may have had the self-motivation to pursue your goal, not all of you had the inner belief that you would succeed.

Belief

The best approach to having inner belief was summed up for me by Venus Williams, Olympic gold medallist in tennis in 2000 and 2008, when she said "You have to be able to believe in yourself when no-one else does — that makes you a winner right there".

Developing your self-efficacy is essential if you are to succeed at the highest level and I have already covered that, in some detail, in the chapter on 'Getting in the zone'.

Research has proved that 'mind games' can enhance your motivation, increase your confidence and self-efficacy, improve your motor performance, prime your mind for success, and increase your state of flow.

Researcher Angie LeVan wrote in *Psychology Today*, "Mental imagery impacts many cognitive processes in the brain: motor control, attention, perception, planning, and the memory, so the brain is getting trained for actual performance during visualisation".

I urge you to use 'mind games' that are tailored for you personally, with a coach's help, and will not only increase your self-efficacy but also give you the best possible preparation before you compete.

Self-esteem

From my own experience, as you may have read earlier in the book, self-esteem can be extremely fragile.

I spent many years demolishing my self-esteem by the way I reacted to uncomfortable, or difficult, situations I found myself in, and to comments people made about me.

It took me a long while to build my self-esteem up again using the combination of self-talk and visualisation that I will be describing in the next chapter on 'Mental simulation'.

If you are, or aspire to be, an elite athlete or sports star, I hope that, after the sacrifices you have made, and the hard work that you have put in, you not only feel proud of yourself but also think you deserve the success you are seeking.

I have worked with competitors who have great belief in their ability, and seem to have the self-esteem they need, and yet more often than not their confidence is not at the ideal level.

Confidence

Coaches have long recognised that part of their role is to boost the confidence of the teams and individuals they are working with. Whatever sport you are involved in, I am sure that your coach has worked with you on that aspect, as well as on your technique and physical fitness.

You also have a responsibility to develop your confidence for yourself and you can use 'mind games' to help you do so.

If your coach is working with 'Mindset Priming', they may already have been able to demonstrate to you that they have removed any doubts or concerns about your prospects that may have been lurking in your subconscious.

What doubts or fears did they find? What subconscious sabotage still lurks at the back of your mind? Are you ready for success? Are you ready for the fame that will accompany it? Are you afraid you may lose?

It was Billie Jean King (winner of 39 Grand Slam tennis titles) who famously said "A champion is afraid of losing. Everyone else is afraid of winning".

In my own case, I recognised some years ago that I had been limiting myself with the conflicting thoughts that, while I wanted to be outstanding, I did not want to stand out.

My self-esteem was not sufficiently high for me to be comfortable with the idea of public acclaim and was therefore holding me back from fulfilling my potential.

Just recently, I recognised that, while I was confident that I was the right person to pioneer this approach, I needed to develop the self-esteem to be able to handle any success and publicity that may follow from my doing so.

I wonder if you know how high your self-efficacy is right now in your particular field of endeavour?

If you are an elite competitor are you aspiring to win a gold medal in the Olympics, or is your conscious self-efficacy limiting you to pursuing a national title?

As I have mentioned earlier in the book, the first 'Mindset Priming' sessions I had with Olympic prospects lived up to my expectations, in that, in every case, the athlete's inner self-efficacy was greater than their current aspiration.

Self-efficacy is so vital to those with high aspirations and I urge you to keep developing your belief, self-esteem and confidence (preferably by working quietly inside your head rather than noisily and boastfully out loud).

I am convinced that even the 15% of you who are instinctively successful will be limiting your aspirations (high as they may be) by not recognising your inner self-efficacy.

I described, at the start of the book, the £1,000 challenge I have issued to coaches, and sports psychologists, to show me a competitor who is (without the help of my approach) already stretching for a goal that is at the limit of their *inner* self-efficacy, and at the same time has zero subconscious resistance to the achievement of that goal.

I do not believe anyone will be able to fulfil the requirements to win that challenge (though I will happily pay up if they do).

I do hope lots of 'superstars' will respond to the challenge, as I am keen to keep demonstrating the effectiveness of my approach, at the highest level. The more stars that benefit from it (whether or not they win the challenge) the better known the approach will become and the more coaches, competitors and therapists will be helped to achieve their goals.

I would have relished the opportunity, before the Rio Olympics, of having half an hour each with gold medallists like Jessica Ennis-Hill, Greg Rutherford, or Mo Farah to see whether I could, even by a small margin, increase the belief level in these superstars, and give them even more of a competitive edge, by improving how well they are actually, subconsciously, primed to perform in their events.

If you know any competitors like them, why not invite them to take up my challenge? (It will almost certainly give them that extra edge.)

Dealing with fear

For many people fear of failure has stopped them pursuing their goals.

With little or no commitment to their aspiration it is likely that they have failed to spot, or seize, opportunities and have then justified their lack of ambition with their lack of success.

If only they had been able to tap into their inner self-efficacy they might well have found a high enough level of inner confidence to be able to overcome their fear of failure.

Rather than fearing failure I recommend that you focus on reaching your goals and adopt the attitude that any setbacks you encounter, en route to achieving your aspirations, will be merely temporary.

I hope none of you have the misfortune, as Goldie Sayers did just before the 2012 Olympics, to incur an injury that prevents you from competing.

Having just broken the British record, with the best throw seen in the world that year, she damaged her throwing arm so badly that she did not manage to reach the final in her home Olympics, having been the favourite.

Being the determined competitor she is, she took

that as a temporary setback and immediately set her sights on achieving a medal in the 2016 Games in Rio.

I am not sure if this next example illustrates my own fear of failure, lack of self-efficacy, a comfort zone issue, or all three.

In the mid-1970s, I co-founded a business in London that grew within a few years to have five offices and two additional partners. It was decided that, strategically, it was timely to have an office in Hong Kong and my partners unanimously turned to me and suggested that I was the one ideally suited to go there to open the new office.

They were astonished when I flatly rejected the suggestion.

I had past experience of starting a business from scratch, of opening an office from scratch, of bringing an office in line with the systems and culture of our partnership, and I was very comfortable managing an office.

Perhaps because I had no knowledge of Hong Kong, perhaps because, as far as I was aware, I had no friends in Hong Kong, and perhaps because I was happily enjoying a social life based in my own home in London, the prospect of moving to Hong Kong to take up that challenge absolutely horrified me.

If, in those days, I had had access to someone doing 'Mindset Priming', I would no doubt have discovered both the level of my unconscious enthusiasm for opening the office and also my subconscious resistance to that idea. I am pretty sure that the resistance would have been 100% (and possibly very difficult to shift) even if there had been a decent level of enthusiasm.

Over the last 30 years it has been interesting to listen to my clients reflecting on the picture of their ideal future that has emerged from their unconscious. Very often (before we have worked on the resistance in the back of their mind) they have come up with all sorts of reasons why they doubt they will be able to make the changes needed to be able to enjoy their ideal future.

In case you are absorbing this without yet having read the rest of the book, I want to make sure you understand why such thoughts and reactions are not only unhelpful but are massively counterproductive.

In the next chapter I am going to describe in great detail how you can use visualisation to help you achieve your aims. I'm also going to encourage you to visualise (in the sense of having a full mental dress rehearsal of you enjoying the success you are seeking) your achievement of your final goal, and of any contributory elements that will help you to get there.

I am going to stress how important it is that your thoughts and comments (your self-talk) support your ambition rather than emphasise your current achievements.

Actions steps for you to take:

Be careful to develop your self-esteem.

Get your coach to check the subconscious level of your self-belief with 'Mindset Priming' or 'Escalating Coaching'.

Boost your confidence by getting your coach to ensure that your goal is within (albeit at the upper limit of) your self-efficacy.

Keep your subconscious drive, energy and creativity working at the optimum level by constantly stretching your goals.

Mental simulation

The key points:

'Mind games' have been a natural and instinctive process for you all your life.

Understanding 'mental simulation' will enable you to control your 'mind games' and ensure they are working effectively for you and moving you steadily towards your objectives.

Repeatedly visualising yourself at the level of performance you are seeking, or needing, is like having a full dress rehearsal of that performance, over and over, so that the performance itself becomes natural for you.

There are different ways to trigger a consistent and appropriate picture/experience in your mind – you need to find the one that works best for you.

Your instinctive change process

Many of the changes in your life that you have achieved, or experienced, thus far will have resulted from your anticipating the new circumstances that you wanted to enjoy, using visualisation to adjust your comfort zone, and then finding you are able to revel in the changes you have achieved.

Effective visualisation involves much more than just thinking about how you want to perform in your next competition. Successful competitors, when using visualisation, truly sense their event taking place in their mind's eye.

As mentioned, Michael Phelps, the greatest swimmer in the history of the Olympics, visualises his ideal swim before he goes to sleep each night.

David Hemery, who set a world record for the 400 metres hurdles when winning Olympic Gold in Mexico in 1968, told me recently "In my own competitive days it was vital for me that I didn't hope to win, I **intended** to win, and visualised that, in huge detail, hundreds of times".

Sports psychologist Dr JoAnn Dahlkoetter wrote in the *Huffington Post* about a speed skater she works with. Her article gave a great description of the range of sensations it helps to involve in visualisation. "She feels her forefoot pushing off the track, she hears the sound of her skates, she sees herself surging ahead of the competition, she experiences all the elements of her race in explicit detail before executing her performance."

One of the key reasons this is an effective process is that fortunately for us, our subconscious does not register the difference between something that is very vividly imagined (perhaps in a 'realistic' dream) and something that we actually experience.

Strange as it may sound, and very fortunately for us, as far as our subconscious is concerned, both events are 'experienced', and stored, as if they actually happened to us.

Effective mental simulation uses experiential imagery to create events that feel as if they have actually happened to us. Repetition of such images stacks up multiple 'experiences' in our subconscious, of things being how we want them to be.

I explained earlier how Gestalt kicks in to help us restore order when reality conflicts with what we want, or expect, to see. When we use visualisation effectively we trigger Gestalt, because the process confronts our subconscious with two conflicting pictures of 'reality'.

Thus, when you vividly and repeatedly imagine that things are already how you want them to be, this is accepted by your subconscious as a picture of actual reality, and that will clearly be in conflict with the genuine reality of the situation, or self-image, that you wish to change. Your subconscious will need to resolve this conflict.

Provided you visualise what you want repeatedly, the picture of your future goal will become the more dominant of the two conflicting pictures. Your subconscious will get creative to move the less dominant picture to match the dominant one and will thereby adapt your self-image, as required, and move you towards the achievement of your goal.

Hopefully you will recognise this as a process you have been using when seeking new standards in competition. Applying the process will achieve the same effect for you as for actors, who repeatedly rehearse for their performance on stage, so that they actually perform, on the day, in a way that they feel they have experienced many times before and that comes quite naturally to them.

Pilots are prepared for duty by being trained in simulators to deal with a whole range of crises that could crop up in an actual flight. They learn, and practise, the appropriate responses so that, should a drama occur in mid-air, they are able to instantly and automatically react without needing to think about which procedure to adopt.

Even without being aware of the technique, we have all used it instinctively. We describe many of the things we automatically do well as 'second nature for us now'.

What made them 'second nature'; how did we shift from what had been 'first nature' for us? It was almost certainly by using mental simulation to speed up the process of assimilating the new behaviour.

Perhaps before you were big enough to ride a tricycle, you observed older children doing so, and thought to yourself "I am nearly old enough to ride a trike" and imagined yourself pedalling away.

Then, once you were old enough to ride your trike, maybe you began imagining yourself riding a bike, then a motor bike, or driving your first car, and so on.

Each acquired technique becomes second nature to you once you have repeatedly imagined yourself doing it, learnt the skills needed, and experienced the reality a few times.

Lasting change starts on the inside in your imagination.

It is worth repeating that when you launch the process by repeatedly visualising, in an experiential way, how you want things to be, you imprint that picture into your subconscious as an existing 'reality'.

When that picture conflicts with the current reality that you are seeking to change, it will trigger tremendous drive, energy and creativity in your subconscious to bring about the change you want – you will be 'putting your mind to it' in the most productive way possible.

The more clearly you define your objectives, the more precisely defined will be the picture you paint in your mind, and the more likely you are to achieve exactly what you want.

Remember also that the greater the gap between your current situation and your aspiration, the more your drive, energy and creativity will be generated subconsciously to make the pictures match.

A full dress rehearsal

To move you on from the theory of how to change to the practical application of that process, I hope you have understood that the easiest and most natural way to achieve your goals is to change 'from the inside out'.

You can best achieve that by imagining how you want to be in the future, imprinting that picture on your subconscious – in such a way that it gradually adjusts your self-concept – and thereby effecting a lasting, and comfortable, change in your behaviour.

There is no limit to how many changes you are able to work on at any one time.

I want you to recognise that you are likely to need to visualise a number of aspects of each goal that you have in mind and that you will need to support the change process, by being careful about the thoughts you allow to run through your mind and the way you describe your performance to others (and in your own head).

To explain these important aspects I would like to move from an emphasis on athletics to the idea of a golfer improving their handicap. The principles I will be describing can be related to any activity or sport.

Let us imagine you are an amateur player with a handicap of 16 and your goal is to get that handicap into single figures. You might think, from what you have been reading, that I'm suggesting that to achieve this change all you need to do is to visualise yourself, at the end of a round of golf, looking at your scorecard and seeing the evidence that you have gone round the course in nine over par.

This would be asking far too much of your subconscious.

I know that if I want to improve my golf game I need to look at its component parts and identify specific aspects to work on: I need to practise and play more often. I need coaching to help me improve my technique when playing out of a bunker. I certainly need to improve my accuracy when chipping onto the green, and I need to work on my line and length when putting.

In making an action plan to improve my golf, I would need to work out how often I wanted to play and practise, and when I would find time to do so. I would need to book lessons with the pro to get help with my bunker shots. Having put these sessions into my diary I would need to start working on my self-image.

At least twice a day I would need to make time for my mental simulation of each of the elements of my game that I am trying to improve. To make the visualisation as realistic as possible, I might imagine myself playing accurate shots on some of the holes on the golf course I regularly play on.

The more you can 'experience' in your visualisation the positive emotions you would feel, and the actions you would be able to perform, the easier it will be for you to not only 'see yourself' but also 'sense yourself' at the new level.

This 'sensing yourself' is called 'experiential' imagery and the more detailed it is, the more effective your mental simulation will be.

Let me give you an example of what I mean by 'experiential' imagery. If I asked you to film me mowing my lawn and I then watched the film on, say, your iPad, I would be able to 'see myself mowing the lawn'.

But if I was to use 'experiential' imagery to 'see myself mowing the lawn' I would see and feel my hands on the back of the mower, see my feet coming into the bottom of the picture in turn, see the immaculate stripes where I had already cut the grass, see the longer grass still ahead of me, smell the new mown grass cuttings, hear the sound of the mower and perhaps birds circling overhead, feel the breeze on my face, etc.

Using 'experiential' imagery involves as many senses as are appropriate for each situation you need to visualise.

There are different techniques for triggering these pictures that I will come to shortly, but I want to stress something very important at this stage. Once you have decided on the performance that you wish to make 'like you' – that is to say the performance you see yourself consistently achieving in the future – it is really important that your thoughts, and the words you use, support this new performance.

To illustrate this in the context of my golf example, if I am visualising myself as a single handicap golfer (chipping well, putting well, and getting out of bunkers when I need to), I will undo all the benefits of visualisation if I allow myself to talk about being 'hopeless at chipping, usually taking three putts, dreading having to get out of bunkers' and so on.

Those kinds of comments would present pictures to my subconscious that add weight to the current reality rather than the future goal.

A very helpful image that sticks in my mind, from one of The Pacific Institute®'s courses, is that of an old-fashioned set of weighing scales (where the item to be weighed was put on one side, and differing weights then added to the other side, until the balance revealed the item's weight).

When I first attended one of their courses I needed to do a lot of work on my self-esteem. In the context of the weighing scales, it was suggested that throughout my life I had frequently been 'putting myself down' and that each time I had done so I had put a negative weight on one side of the scales. I realised that over the years these weights had accumulated to ensure that I leant in that negative direction.

To reverse that damage I was taught to stop loading the negative side and start putting positive weights on the other side of the scales. I mentally covered up the pile of negatives, realised I could use visualisation to put positive weights on the other side, and recognised also that I could reinforce the change I wanted by ensuring that my self-talk was positive and supportive at all times.

While this book is primarily written for aspiring sports stars and their coaches, I would encourage you, should you choose to adopt this technique, to apply it widely to every aspect of your life and not just to your career or ambitions.

I suggest you take a piece of paper, or type yourself some notes on your computer or iPad, listing aspects of your life that are not as you would ideally like them to be.

Then prioritise the improvements you would like to see and practise applying the following techniques to achieve your aims.

Techniques for triggering mental simulation

By now I am sure that you understand the need to imprint a consistent picture, in your subconscious, of you reveling in the achievement of your objectives.

When appropriate, and possible, it is brilliant to relive an actual experience in your mind (as Steve Backley did after visiting Helsinki), perhaps adding a new or better outcome if necessary.

When that option is not available some people like to use photographs, or images cut from magazines, to imprint the picture.

Others prefer to write a carefully worded sentence that gives them a sense of experiencing the achievement and being filled with appropriate emotions. Such a sentence is often referred to as an 'affirmation'.

Any of these approaches will clearly ensure that each time you visualise you will consistently be imprinting the same picture into your subconscious. That is important because you need a consistent picture if your visualisation is to trigger ongoing conflict with your current reality.

Writing affirmations

If you choose to use affirmations, the simplest way to write them is to use a four step process: first, describe what you want to change about yourself or your situation; second, write down how you would like life or success to be instead; third, turn that description into a first person, present tense sentence that includes reference to the benefit you will have gained by making that adjustment; finally, write any supporting affirmations that will be needed.

When I started using the affirmation process, I found my sentences were often quite long. With time, I learnt that very often the shorter the sentence the more powerful it could be.

Many books have been published on techniques for writing affirmations and they very often list eight or more elements that need to be included if an affirmation is to be successful.

That approach works fine but is not always necessary.

The most powerful affirmation I have ever seen was just three words long.

I was shown it during a workshop that I was running a while ago when one of the participants asked me for help with his affirmations. He was somewhat round-shouldered, stooping, and prematurely grey. He also lacked confidence and told me he had low self-esteem. He was concerned that the affirmation he had written did not meet all the criteria that I had suggested could be helpful.

Whenever I tell this story I find myself welling up, because when I read his affirmation to myself I immediately realised that it was brilliant.

I asked him to read it out loud for me and his affirmation simply was, simply, "I walk tall". As he spoke it he visibly straightened up, his shoulders went back, and he stood up straight.

Of course, he needed to do more than use that one affirmation if he was going to successfully rebuild his self-esteem, but it was a great start and would do wonders for helping him hold his head up with pride.

Having shared that with you, here are some of the recommendations for writing affirmations effectively that are often quoted and that I hope you will find helpful.

Guidelines for success with affirmations

You will need to write an affirmation for each of your goals in the first person, present tense – as if it is a reality NOW, *i.e. "I feel wonderful hearing the crowds cheering as I stand on the Olympic podium with the gold medal round my neck".*

Using language that describes your potential, rather than the success you are aspiring to, will not work for you and you will want to avoid any sentences like *"I can run the 100 metres in under 10 seconds".*

If you are a runner, because your event may be affected by differing track conditions or headwinds, affirming that you *always* succeed in achieving a particular time is not recommended either because your subconscious will be aware that the statement is not likely to be true. So also avoid affirming anything like *"I always run the 100 metres in under 10 seconds"*.

If you're currently running 100 metres in over 10 seconds, and genuinely think you have the talent and determination to be the best in the business, an affirmation you might think would work for you could be: *"I'm proud to have broken 10 seconds for the 100 metres and I'm really looking forward to breaking the British record"*.

However that is not a great affirmation either, firstly because there are two separate achievements referred to (and you want to give your subconscious one picture per affirmation) and importantly, also, the second achievement is one you are looking forward to (i.e. it is in the future) and you need to picture things in the present to achieve the conflict with your actual reality.

"I'm proud to have broken 10 seconds for the 100 metres" might do for one affirmation (though it sounds a bit flat, or bland, and non-specific to me) while the second half of the original version would need to read something like *"I feel over the moon to be the British 100 metres record holder"*.

It would be even better to be specific about the time you are intending to achieve. In your visualisation you might want to see that time up in lights, against your name, on the giant scoreboard.

Strange as it may sound I hope you don't choose to use any of the sample affirmations that you see here. The reason I say that is that they are written using my words rather than yours.

If you're going to use affirmations the words need to be your own – in every sense sounding like you.

The late Pat Given, one of the great mentors in my life, was helping a group with their affirmations and one of the participants was something of a rough diamond whose habit was to litter his sentences with some pretty robust swear words. Presenting his affirmations to Pat, he had stated they were useless and didn't work. Pat read them and pointed out that they were written in surprisingly elegant English prose (rather than in the more robust language that the individual normally used). Pat encouraged the man to write his affirmations incorporating his usual way of speaking, which he was sure would work better for the individual concerned.

Several weeks later Pat got a telephone call from the man who, using a typical number of swear words, told him gleefully how great affirmations were and how well they were working now he littered them with four-letter words.

So create affirmations, written in your own way of speaking, which inspire you, excite you, and trigger a picture of believable success, and be sure to write each aspiration as if you had already achieved it. Be as specific as possible about the detail of the change, express the benefit of the achievement, include any appropriate emotion about the change and use action words (where suitable) that describe the new experience.

Then 'live' each vision in your mind at least twice a day and experience the event as you would if you were able to practise it in a simulator.

Using supporting affirmations

In Part 3 of the book, in the chapter on 'Escalating Coaching', I described how I had helped a golfer to recognise that he had the talent to be far more accurate with some of his clubs than he had realised. To achieve that level of accuracy consistently he, of course, needed to change his self-image and his self-talk. So, since his overall goal was to reduce his handicap and turn pro, he would have needed to have an affirmation about playing as a professional, and also to have supporting affirmations about the consistent accuracy he achieved with each of his clubs.

In Part 2 of the book, I suggested that the four things that hold us back from achieving our objectives are beliefs, expectations, habits, and attitudes.

In helping people to achieve their goals, I always suggest that, having set the goal and written their main affirmation, the next stage is to identify any of those four blocking elements that might hold them back. They then need to write supporting affirmations to change the belief, the habit, or whatever combination of blockers they think are impeding their progress.

If you are an athlete and compete in more than one event, perhaps a heptathlete or decathlete, you may also need supporting affirmations about improving some of your techniques.

You may have an overall affirmation about winning a gold medal and you may need supporting affirmations about your take-off (when jumping), getting out of your blocks (when sprinting), or your field event prowess.

If you are a golfer, you may need supporting affirmations about a number of the clubs that you use, or aspects of your game that you are working on.

The more you can think of affirmations that will support your achievement of your goals, the easier it will be for your subconscious to adjust your self-image so that you free-flow at the new level.

You have almost certainly used the mental simulation process to bring about change instinctively before. You now know how to control it.

Gradual and incremental change

With this approach you can change attitudes and expectations quite quickly. Beliefs and habits are likely to take longer. All changes tend to be gradual and incremental but will be sustainable.

One thing I would like to emphasise is that it is important to be patient and allow the change in your self-image to be the source of the change in your performance.

What that means is that you do not give up, or stop doing, something immediately (which you may have done in the past when you made a New Year's resolution).

If you forcibly change your natural and instinctive behaviour (rather than waiting for the change to come about from your adjusted self-image) it will stimulate your subconscious to get you back to being 'like you'.

Instead, with this approach, you decide on the change you want to make, frequently visualise the 'you' that you wish to become (imprinting that picture on your subconscious) which will change your self-image which will then, in turn, change your natural and instinctive behaviour into how you wish it to be.

In other words, you just let the 'mind games' do their work and carry on being you.

Controlling your self-talk

I have mentioned before how important it is that your self-talk is in line with your aspirations and affirmations.

If you go back to my example of the weighing scales, I think it will be easy for you to see that if you use an affirmation to bring about change (effectively putting a positive weight on one side of the scales) you will cancel out the benefit of that if you allow your self-talk to put a contradictory picture on the other side of the scales.

"I'm happy that my technique is improving" or some such comment will support your affirmations in that direction, whereas, "I am still lousy at ..." most certainly will not.

Talking of weighing scales, people often use visualisation to achieve a healthier weight.

As a fit athlete this is unlikely to be a change you need to make but someone in your family may appreciate some coaching from you in this direction.

I have often been asked to help people get thinner and very often I'm told that they have no trouble losing the weight but always put it back on again. If I ask them what they did with their old clothes (having lost the weight in the first place), I can guarantee they tell me that they put them in the back of a cupboard, or in the loft or garage. The reason for this is that in their mind they knew they would need the clothes again when they had put the weight back on. In other words, their self-image had not changed and they still saw themselves as a larger person.

It is preferable not to use self-talk such as, "I'm trying to lose weight" because 'trying to' conveys an expectation of failure. If someone you know is working on losing weight, then suitable self-talk for them could be, "I'm looking forward to having more energy" or "I'm going to find it much easier to get around the golf course" or even "I can't wait to take all these clothes to the charity shop and replace them with something that flatters the new me". (Please note that these sentences using the future tense are fine for your self-talk but would not work as affirmations because those need to be in the present tense if they are to have the desired impact.)

It really helps, if wanting to lose weight, if your affirmations refer to the benefit you will gain from being lighter ('now I run when out walking the dog', 'having more energy', 'looking great in the mirror', etc.).

Once I added the 'benefit' words to my affirmations I found they had much more impact – I strongly recommend you to try it.

The self-talk spiral

Once you recognise how your self-talk develops your
self-image, and the link between that and your
performance, then I am sure you will see the value in
paying careful attention to how you talk to you.

From now on listen to your self-talk and make
sure it is helping you towards your objectives.

Successful people talk themselves into success
with an ongoing upward spiral. Many people talk
themselves out of success and watch their performance
spiral downwards. Both groups use a process of
comment –self-image – performance – comment – self-
image etc. The only difference is whether the
comment/self-talk sends the spiral upwards or
downwards.

What you need to do, having set your aspirational
goal, is to align your self-talk with that goal and then
mentally rehearse that achievement.

En route to your success there may be days when
your performance falls short of expectations. On those
days, it is important to say to yourself something like
"that's not like me, I'm better than that, the next time I
will get it right".

On days when you exceed your expectations you
might want to say something like "I'm getting better all
the time and next week I look forward to... throwing
even further / running even faster / getting more pars
(or birdies)" – preferably naming specific distances and
times.

Prepare for an endless journey

The two most frequent reasons I have heard people use,
for resisting the idea of change, are that they anticipate

172

firstly that the process would be stressful and secondly that the changes would not last.

I hope I have explained why using mental simulation *will* help you achieve the changes you are seeking to make.

I hope it also makes sense when I assure you that, if you do use that approach, your progress towards your goals will be *comfortable*, because it will be achieved by you changing your self-image, and reinforced by you using appropriate self-talk, while just behaving in a natural and free-flowing way.

If that makes sense to you, then you do not need me to explain why, once your self-image has been adjusted to the 'new you', that will underpin the new behaviour and your changes will be *sustainable* (until such time as you may choose to set new goals or targets).

As I have suggested earlier, there may be setbacks along the way. You can prepare for them by deciding what sort of thought process you will adopt, in the event of a disappointment, and mentally rehearse that response so that you can pick yourself up and get back on track quickly.

I hope both your career and your life will flourish and become more enjoyable now you have the 'mind games' you need to help you on your journey to a happier, more fulfilling and successful future.

There is a lot you can do for yourself and by now you know that there is a lot a coach, or sports psychologist, can do to support you with 'Escalating Coaching' or 'Mindset Priming'.

So go for it!

"If it's to be, it's up to me"

In quoting this well-known saying I am simply suggesting that you take accountability for your future.

Aim high and 'put your mind' to making your dreams come true – and get your coach to help you.

You can get more information on where to find mentors trained in 'Escalating Coaching' and 'Mindset Priming' from my website: www.pathfindersabc.co.uk.

Coaches and mentors can choose how far they wish to progress with the 'Escalating Coaching' training programme:

Step 1   Insights on The ABC of Success *For those wanting to help clients put their minds to boosting their performance.*

Step 2   Introduction to Muscle Testing & Goal Stretching *For those wanting the basic skills to help clients stretch their goals to the optimum by accessing their <u>inner</u> self-belief.*

Step 3   Introduction to Goal Balancing *For those wanting to reduce their clients' subconscious resistance/sabotage by integrating additional techniques with those gained in Steps 1 & 2.*

Step 4   Introduction to Getting in the Zone & Mind/Body alignment *For those wanting further techniques with which to correct some physical/energetic imbalances (perhaps caused by trauma) and mentally prepare clients for success.*

These 4 introductory steps progressively increase a coach's ability to help their clients and protégés with 'Mindset Priming'. I would be happy to recommend suitable Kinesiology training, that provides a wider range of techniques, to coaches wanting to work with Escalating Coaching at an even more profound level.

Actions steps for you to take:

Make a list of any aspects of your life, career, or future prospects, that you would like to improve.

For each one, describe the best you could possibly imagine that aspect could be.

Make an action plan of steps you will need to take, or skills you will need to gain, in order to reach that 'pinnacle of success'.

Think whether there are any of your existing beliefs, expectations, habits or attitudes that might be holding you back – then identify what the replacement would need to be.

Choose what you think will be the best trigger for regular and consistent mental simulation of you enjoying each success or change.

Find the time for a full 'dress rehearsal' of each picture at least twice a day.

If possible, get help from your coach to fine-tune the choices you have made.

(You can find how to contact those trained in this approach via my website:
www.pathfindersabc.co.uk)

February 2017

Postscript to this revised edition

Dear Reader

If you have read this far you have presumably found some part(s) of the book interesting or helpful.

Since publishing the original edition I have been overwhelmed by the level of interest expressed in my integrated approach and I have already introduced this new concept to sports coaches working with athletes (track and field), golfers, cricketers, tennis players and footballers.

As you will have read, the first edition of the book was written with such competitors and their coaches in mind.

Although a much wider audience is now expressing interest in 'Mindset Priming' I decided not to do a substantial rewrite for this revised edition, but instead simply to bring the book up-to-date factually.

This gave me much more time to get on with what I am passionate about – sharing what I know with others (and not just coaches, and trainers) who want to help people, of every description, to fulfil their potential.

I see myself as the Christopher Columbus of the coaching world - responsible for changing 'flat earth' thinking and introducing the world to the idea of being able to go much deeper with 'Mindset Priming'.

I see it as my job to intrigue people with the thought that they can easily learn how to turn coaching inside-out and help those in their care to listen to their own inner voice (rather than listening to their coach's beliefs).

Having now broken down 'Escalating Coaching' into the four steps described on the revised page 174, I have made it as easy as I can for coaches and mentors (of every kind) to gain those techniques that they see as being relevant to the level of support they want to give their clients.

So many adults, who I have introduced to the concepts in step 1 of 'Mindset Priming', have commented "Why did no one teach me this at school?" that I would also like to arrange, or run, workshops for parenting groups, teachers, and community groups, in addition to those I am holding for businesses and coaches.

Launching this new approach feels like a mammoth undertaking and I would really appreciate any help you can give me in finding likeminded people who have a responsibility to mentor others.

One way you could help is by directing them to this book's website: www.theinsidetrack.guru, where they can find out more about my approach by downloading the free extracts.

Also, if you know any sports competitors, please direct them to the same site, because many have told me how much they need support with their mental preparation and I hope, and think, that they will be very likely to find the complete, and free, download on 'mental simulation' (taken from the "mind games" section of this book) of real help in their future careers.

You probably gathered from the book that I am also really hopeful that my work will benefit Help for Heroes patients and Invictus Games competitors. I'm looking for any opportunity to demonstrate the potential of this approach to those working with traumatised people, so please, if you have any connections in that world, do encourage them to contact me, or refer them to this book and its website.

The best way I can help people (including our potential sports stars) is to make it easy for their coaches to get whatever mindset training appeals to them.

There are already many people around the country who I consider qualified to teach some of the basic steps of 'Mindset Priming' and I will happily direct coaches to their closest instructors, once I know which steps they wish to take.

For those of you wanting more information about my work my business website: www.pathfindersabc.co.uk will gives you a fuller picture, information on finding coaches who have been trained in this approach, and workshops that are available.

Thank you for your interest and for any ongoing support you can provide.

With my best wishes

Jeremy

Lightning Source UK Ltd.
Milton Keynes UK
UKOW05f0133010317
295600UK00001B/23/P